I0783103

Government Wasteful Spending:

A Taxpayer's Nightmare

Samuel Carter

This book is a work of non-fiction. While every effort has been made to ensure accuracy, the author and publisher assume no responsibility for errors or omissions or for consequences arising from the use of the information contained herein.

Published by Samuel Carter

First Edition: December 2024
Printed in the United States of America

Table of Contents:

IIntroduction: Purpose and Overview

Government spending is a fundamental function of governance, intended to provide public goods and services that promote economic stability, national security, and societal well-being. However, when mismanaged, this spending can spiral into wastefulness, diverting precious taxpayer dollars away from critical needs. Wasteful spending not only undermines public trust but also exacerbates pressing issues such as national debt, economic inequality, and inadequate infrastructure.

The goal of this book, Government Wasteful Spending: A Taxpayer's Nightmare, is to shine a light on the scope and impact of wasteful government practices, drawing from documented cases and credible sources. This exploration is not merely an exercise in critique; it is a call to action for reform, advocating for greater transparency, accountability, and fiscal responsibility in governance.

Defining the Problem
Wasteful government spending encompasses a range of activities, from frivolous projects to systemic mismanagement and fraud. It occurs at all levels of governance—federal, state, and local—and affects virtually every sector, from defense and healthcare to education and environmental programs. Some of the most egregious examples, such as multimillion-dollar research projects with questionable relevance or misallocated pandemic relief funds, reveal a troubling lack of oversight and prioritization.

Understanding wasteful spending requires more than identifying absurd projects. It necessitates an examination of the systems and

policies that allow such inefficiencies to persist. By delving into the "why" and "how" behind these practices, this book aims to uncover root causes and propose actionable solutions.
Why Wasteful Spending Matters
Government budgets are funded by taxpayers who expect their contributions to be utilized effectively and responsibly. Every dollar

wasted represents an opportunity lost—an unmet need in education, healthcare, infrastructure, or other critical areas. Wasteful spending affects everyone, but its impacts are particularly severe for vulnerable populations who rely on government services.

For instance, consider the national debt, which currently exceeds $30 trillion. Wasteful spending contributes significantly to this staggering figure, limiting the government's ability to invest in long-term priorities like clean energy, affordable housing, and public health initiatives. The ripple effects include higher taxes, reduced public services, and economic instability.

Moreover, the perception of waste damages public trust in government institutions. When citizens learn of projects like $1 million spent on shrimp treadmill experiments or $43 million gas stations in remote locations, skepticism about governmental priorities grows. This erosion of trust can lead to reduced civic engagement and voter apathy, weakening the very fabric of democracy.

The Broader Implications of Mismanagement
While specific examples of wasteful spending are often attention-grabbing, they reflect deeper issues within the systems and structures of governance. Bureaucratic inefficiencies, lack of oversight, and political incentives to fund "pet projects" create an environment where wasteful practices flourish.

For example, many government programs are designed without clear benchmarks for success or mechanisms for evaluating their effectiveness. As a result, funds are often allocated based on tradition or political expediency rather than demonstrated need or impact. This mismanagement not only wastes money but also undermines the effectiveness of programs intended to address critical challenges, such as poverty alleviation or climate change.

Examples of Egregious Waste
While wasteful spending spans every sector, certain cases stand out as particularly egregious, illustrating the magnitude of the issue and its underlying causes. These examples are not isolated incidents but symptoms of broader systemic inefficiencies.

$1 Million on Shrimp on a Treadmill:
This infamous example of questionable research spending involved a study funded by the National Science Foundation (NSF) to observe shrimp running on a treadmill. While proponents argued that the study had ecological relevance, it quickly became a symbol of frivolous spending in federal research programs.

$43 Million Gas Station in Afghanistan:
A single compressed natural gas (CNG) fueling station built as part of a U.S. reconstruction effort in Afghanistan cost taxpayers an astonishing $43 million. Auditors later revealed that the project could have been completed for less than $1 million, highlighting poor planning and oversight.

Pandemic Relief Fraud:
The COVID-19 pandemic necessitated rapid disbursement of relief funds, but the lack of safeguards led to widespread fraud. Billions of dollars intended for small businesses and unemployed individuals were siphoned off by criminals exploiting loopholes in the system.

These examples, while varied in their specifics, share commonalities: inadequate oversight, misplaced priorities, and a lack of accountability. They underscore the need for systemic reform to prevent similar occurrences in the future.

A Call for Accountability
The examples outlined above are not simply amusing anecdotes or isolated instances of mismanagement—they represent a deeper failure to prioritize the needs of citizens and steward public funds responsibly. To address these issues, we must demand accountability at all levels of governance.

Accountability begins with transparency. Citizens must have access to clear, detailed information about how their tax dollars are spent. Advocacy organizations and watchdog groups play a crucial role in monitoring government spending and exposing waste. Policymakers, in turn, must commit to enacting reforms that emphasize performance metrics, oversight, and efficient use of resources.

The Objectives of This Book
The purpose of Government Wasteful Spending: A Taxpayer's
Nightmare is twofold: to expose the extent and consequences of
wasteful government spending and to provide actionable solutions
for reform. This book draws on real-world examples, credible reports, and expert analysis to offer a comprehensive exploration of
the issue.

1. Educating the Public:
Many citizens are unaware of how pervasive wasteful spending is
or how it impacts their daily lives. By highlighting absurd projects,
bureaucratic inefficiencies, and systemic failures, this book aims to
inform readers and foster a deeper understanding of the problem.

2. Encouraging Advocacy:
Public pressure is one of the most effective drivers of change.
When citizens demand greater accountability, governments are
compelled to respond. This book provides tools and strategies for
advocacy, empowering readers to take an active role in holding
their leaders accountable.

3. Offering Solutions:
Exposing waste is only the first step; identifying and implementing
solutions is the ultimate goal. This book outlines a roadmap for reform, addressing both systemic changes and practical policies that
can reduce waste and improve efficiency.

How This Book Is Structured
This book is divided into five parts, each focusing on a specific aspect of government waste and accountability:

Part I: Understanding Government Waste: Explores the definitions,
causes, and consequences of wasteful spending, providing a foundational understanding of the issue.
Part II: Absurd Projects and Grants: Delves into some of the most
notorious examples of waste, from shrimp treadmills to overseas
cultural programs.
Part III: Widespread Bureaucratic Failures: Examines systemic inefficiencies in major institutions like the Pentagon and Medicare, as

well as failures in pandemic relief programs.
Part IV: Mismanagement in Federal and Local Programs: Highlights inefficiencies in infrastructure projects, education spending, and local government initiatives.
Part V: Solutions and a Path Forward: Offers actionable recommendations for reform, focusing on the roles of policymakers, watchdog organizations, and citizen advocacy.
Each chapter is designed to build on the previous one, providing readers with a comprehensive understanding of the issue and a clear path forward.

A Vision for Change
The goal of this book extends beyond merely identifying problems—it seeks to inspire a collective movement toward accountability and reform. By understanding the patterns and systems that enable wasteful spending, readers will be better equipped to advocate for effective governance. The vision is clear: a government that uses every taxpayer dollar wisely, focuses on measurable outcomes, and prioritizes the needs of its citizens.

This vision is not unattainable. Around the world and within the United States, there are examples of governments and organizations that have successfully reformed their practices to eliminate waste and foster transparency. These models provide hope and a blueprint for change.

A Call to Readers
As you embark on this journey through the pages of Government Wasteful Spending: A Taxpayer's Nightmare, consider your role in this larger movement. Whether as a concerned citizen, an advocate, or a policymaker, you have the power to influence change. Here's how you can start:

Stay Informed: Awareness is the first step toward accountability. By understanding how wasteful spending happens and its consequences, you'll be better positioned to advocate for change.
Engage Your Community: Discuss these issues with others and share the knowledge you gain from this book. Collective action starts with individual conversations.
Take Action: Whether it's contacting your representatives, joining

advocacy groups, or participating in local government initiatives, your voice matters.

The Road Ahead

The chapters that follow will take you on a deep dive into the world of government waste, exposing its causes, consequences, and potential solutions. From absurd projects to systemic inefficiencies, you will see how deeply entrenched these practices are and what it will take to uproot them. Most importantly, you will discover that reform is not just possible—it is essential.

Through the examples, analyses, and recommendations in this book, you will gain the tools needed to join the movement for fiscal responsibility. Together, we can demand better governance, reduce waste, and ensure that public funds are used to build a better future for all.

Chapter 1: What Is Wasteful Spending?

Government spending is a fundamental part of how modern nations operate. Through taxation, governments collect funds from citizens to build infrastructure, maintain public safety, fund education, provide healthcare, and deliver other services that are meant to improve the quality of life. However, not all government spending achieves these noble goals. Some projects, programs, and expenditures fail to provide meaningful value to the public. These instances fall into the realm of wasteful spending—a phenomenon that costs taxpayers billions of dollars every year and leaves them wondering where their money truly goes.

Wasteful spending is not merely about errors or oversights in budgeting; it's often the result of systemic inefficiencies, misaligned priorities, and a lack of accountability. The term "wasteful spending" refers to any allocation of public funds that is unnecessary, redundant, poorly managed, or unrelated to the intended purpose of those funds. This broad definition encompasses everything from overpriced contracts to ill-conceived projects and redundant bureaucracies. Wasteful spending doesn't just squander resources—it undermines public trust in government institutions, fueling frustration and skepticism among citizens.

A classic example of wasteful spending comes from the infamous "bridge to nowhere" in Alaska. The project, which would have cost taxpayers $398 million, aimed to connect the town of Ketchikan (population: 8,000) to Gravina Island (population: 50). While infrastructure development is critical, the project's astronomical cost compared to its limited utility led to widespread public criticism. Ultimately, the bridge was never built, and the funds were redirected, but not before the proposal became a symbol of government waste and misplaced priorities.

What Makes Spending Wasteful?

To truly grasp the scope of wasteful spending, it's important to understand how it is identified. While the term can evoke images of blatant misuse, such as fraud or embezzlement, wasteful spending is often more subtle. A project may have good intentions but fail to deliver measurable benefits. Alternatively, spending may align with a specific agenda but lack a clear purpose or justification for its cost. Watchdog organizations like the Government Accountability Office (GAO) and independent reports such as Senator Rand Paul's Festivus Report have developed criteria for identifying wasteful spending:

Is the expenditure necessary? Does the spending address a pressing need or solve an identifiable problem?
Are the costs reasonable? Could the same goals be achieved at a lower expense?
What is the public benefit? Is the outcome of the spending measurable, meaningful, and beneficial to taxpayers?
These questions form the foundation for evaluating whether a given expenditure constitutes waste. For instance, in 2017, the federal government allocated over $1.3 million to study whether Americans would eat ground-up insects as a protein source. While sustainable food production is a worthy goal, critics questioned whether this specific research warranted such a high investment of taxpayer funds, especially given the more immediate issues facing the nation at the time.

The Festivus Report often highlights examples like this to illustrate how even seemingly small expenditures can accumulate into significant sums when multiplied across government departments. These cases not only waste money but also signal a failure to prioritize resources effectively, leaving critical areas like education, healthcare, and infrastructure underfunded.

Why Wasteful Spending Happens
Understanding what constitutes wasteful spending also involves examining the systemic factors that allow it to occur. One major contributor is bureaucratic inefficiency. Government agencies often operate under rigid structures that make it difficult to streamline processes or eliminate redundancies. For example, multiple agencies may be tasked with overlapping responsibilities, leading to duplication of efforts and unnecessary expenditures.

Another factor is the political nature of government spending.

Elected officials often advocate for projects that benefit their constituents or align with their political agendas, even if those projects lack broader merit. Known as "pork-barrel spending," this practice involves directing funds to specific districts or states to secure political support. While this can help officials gain favor with voters, it frequently leads to wasteful projects that serve narrow interests rather than the greater good.

A lack of accountability further exacerbates the problem. Many government programs operate with limited oversight, making it difficult to track how funds are used or measure the effectiveness of spending. In some cases, funds are allocated to programs without clear benchmarks for success, resulting in expenditures that continue year after year without meaningful evaluation. For example, a GAO investigation revealed that the Department of Defense spent over $1 billion on unused spare parts due to poor inventory management. While defense spending is crucial, inefficiencies like these demonstrate how a lack of oversight can lead to significant waste.

The Cost of Mismanagement

The consequences of wasteful spending extend far beyond the individual programs or projects involved. At a time when the national debt exceeds $33 trillion and annual deficits continue to grow, every dollar wasted represents a lost opportunity. Funds that could have been used to repair aging infrastructure, improve public schools, or expand access to healthcare are instead diverted to unnecessary or poorly managed initiatives.

Moreover, wasteful spending erodes public trust in government. Taxpayers expect their contributions to be used responsibly and transparently. When they see reports of frivolous expenditures, it undermines their confidence in the government's ability to manage resources effectively. This erosion of trust can have long-term implications, reducing civic engagement and increasing skepticism toward public institutions.

One of the most striking aspects of wasteful government spending is how it manifests across various sectors. From scientific research grants to military contracts, the problem is not confined to a single area. Instead, it reflects systemic inefficiencies that are difficult to address without major structural reforms. Understanding these manifestations provides a clearer picture of how taxpayer dollars are squandered.

Infamous Examples of Wasteful Spending

Wasteful spending often grabs headlines for its absurdity, but it also serves as a reminder of deeper issues within government operations. Take, for instance, the infamous case of the National Science Foundation spending $3 million on a study to determine if shrimp could run on a treadmill. While the research may have had a narrow scientific purpose, the public backlash was swift, with critics questioning the relevance and cost of such a project.

Another example came to light during the height of the pandemic. In an effort to address the economic fallout, the federal government issued billions in relief funds through programs like the Paycheck Protection Program (PPP). However, a lack of safeguards led to widespread fraud, with reports indicating that up to $80 billion of pandemic relief funds were misused. This included fake businesses claiming funds, duplicate applications, and funds being diverted to luxury purchases. While the urgency of the pandemic justified rapid action, the oversight failures highlight a recurring issue in government spending.

The Department of Agriculture provides yet another case study. In recent years, it has funded marketing campaigns for food products that are already widely popular. A $2 million campaign to promote avocados raised eyebrows, as the fruit's rising popularity was evident without the need for taxpayer-funded advertising. Critics argue that such expenditures represent a misuse of resources that could be better allocated to addressing food insecurity or supporting small farmers.

Systemic Issues Behind the Problem

To address wasteful spending, it's necessary to look beyond individual cases and consider the systemic issues that allow such expenditures to persist. Bureaucratic inefficiencies are a key factor. Government agencies often operate in silos, with limited communication or coordination between departments. This can result in overlapping responsibilities, redundant programs, and wasted funds. For example, multiple agencies may be tasked with addressing environmental conservation, leading to duplicated efforts and inefficiencies in resource allocation.

Political incentives also play a significant role. Elected officials often advocate for projects that benefit their constituents, even if those projects lack broader merit. Known as "pork-barrel spending," this practice involves directing funds to specific districts to secure votes or political support. While this can help officials achieve short-term political goals, it frequently leads to wasteful expenditures that serve narrow interests rather than the greater good.

Another contributing factor is the lack of accountability in government spending. Many programs operate without clear benchmarks for success, making it difficult to evaluate their effectiveness. In some cases, funds are allocated to programs that continue year after year without meaningful oversight. This creates a culture where inefficiency is tolerated and even expected, further compounding the problem.

The Impact on Taxpayers

The consequences of wasteful spending are not abstract; they have tangible effects on taxpayers. Every dollar spent on an unnecessary project is a dollar that could have been used to address pressing societal needs. For example, funds wasted on redundant programs could be redirected to repairing crumbling infrastructure, improving public education, or expanding access to healthcare.

Moreover, wasteful spending contributes to the growing national debt, which has now exceeded $33 trillion. As the debt grows, so does the cost of servicing it, with interest payments consuming an increasingly large share of the federal budget. This leaves less room for essential services and increases the financial burden on future generations.

Taxpayers also feel the impact in their daily lives. When public funds are mismanaged, the quality of services they receive often declines. Roads and bridges remain in disrepair, public schools face budget constraints, and healthcare programs struggle to meet demand—all while billions of dollars are spent on projects that provide little to no benefit. This creates a sense of frustration and disillusionment among citizens, who see their hard-earned money being wasted while their needs go unmet.

Public Trust and Civic Engagement

Beyond the financial implications, wasteful spending has a profound impact on public trust in government. When taxpayers see reports of frivolous expenditures, it undermines their confidence in the government's ability to manage resources effectively. This erosion of trust can have long-term consequences, reducing civic engagement and increasing skepticism toward public institutions. Citizens who feel disconnected or disillusioned are less likely to participate in democratic processes, such as voting or advocating for policy changes. This creates a vicious cycle where inefficiency and waste go unchallenged, further perpetuating the problem.

The Call for Reform

Addressing wasteful spending requires more than identifying individual cases; it necessitates systemic changes to how resources are allocated and managed. This includes implementing stricter oversight mechanisms, improving coordination between agencies, and holding officials accountable for mismanagement. By taking these steps, the government can begin to rebuild public trust and ensure that taxpayer dollars are used effectively.

In the next section of this chapter, we will delve deeper into specific examples of wasteful spending from recent years, illustrating how these issues continue to affect taxpayers and the nation as a whole. These cases not only highlight the scope of the problem but also underscore the urgent need for reform.

The breadth of wasteful spending in government is staggering, with examples emerging year after year that defy common sense and highlight glaring inefficiencies. These instances of waste are not confined to one agency or level of government—they span across federal, state, and even local programs. To fully appreciate the magnitude of the issue, we must examine a few more specific and recent cases, each shedding light on how taxpayer dollars are misused.

Case Study: Pentagon Waste and Overspending

The Department of Defense (DoD) is consistently one of the largest areas of federal spending. Its budget, which exceeds $800 billion annually, is vital for maintaining national security. However, it is also plagued by inefficiencies and mismanagement. A 2015 report revealed that the Pentagon had identified $125 billion in bureaucratic waste over a five-year period but suppressed the findings to avoid budget cuts.

One particularly egregious example involved the procurement of spare parts. The DoD spent over $1 billion on parts that were never used, simply because it lacked a centralized system to track inventory. As a result, warehouses were stocked with unnecessary equipment while troops in active combat zones faced shortages of critical supplies. This case illustrates how mismanagement, even in an essential area like defense, can lead to significant waste.

In another instance, the Pentagon was criticized for spending $43 million to construct a gas station in Afghanistan—an amount 140 times higher than what a similar project would have cost in the United States. An investigation later revealed that the excessive costs were due to poor planning and lack of oversight. While ensuring operational capacity in conflict zones is critical, such examples highlight how even well-intentioned initiatives can spiral into wasteful expenditures when not properly managed.

Case Study: Research Projects Gone Awry

Scientific research is a critical driver of innovation, but some federally funded projects raise questions about their relevance and necessity. For example, the National Institutes of Health (NIH) funded a $592,000 study to explore whether chimpanzees could be trained to play video games. While the study may have been of interest to the scientific community, its practical applications were unclear, leading critics to question the justification for such an expense.

Similarly, a $1.3 million grant was awarded to study whether Americans would eat insects as a sustainable food source. While the concept of alternative protein sources has merit, many taxpayers questioned whether this specific study was the best use of public funds, especially when food insecurity remains a pressing issue for millions of Americans.

These examples are not just isolated incidents—they reflect a broader trend of research funding that often prioritizes niche academic interests over practical societal benefits. While innovation should be encouraged, a lack of clear benchmarks for evaluating the impact of research spending allows waste to proliferate.

Case Study: Local Government Failures

Wasteful spending is not limited to the federal government. State and local governments also contribute to the problem, often in ways that directly affect communities. For example, in 2021, a city council in California allocated $6.9 million for a bike lane project that was ultimately abandoned after public backlash. The funds, which could have been used for road repairs or other infrastructure improvements, were wasted due to poor planning and lack of community input.

In another case, a small town in Michigan spent $4.5 million on a water treatment facility that was never completed because of a failure to secure necessary permits. The abandoned facility now stands as a monument to inefficiency, with taxpayers left to cover the cost.

Local government waste can be especially frustrating for citizens because the impact is often immediate and visible. When public funds are mismanaged at this level, it directly affects the quality of life in communities, from delayed road repairs to underfunded schools and emergency services.

The Ripple Effect of Waste

Beyond the immediate costs, wasteful spending has long-term implications for the nation. Every dollar squandered on unnecessary projects or mismanaged programs adds to the national debt, which continues to grow at an alarming rate. The current debt burden exceeds $33 trillion, with interest payments alone accounting for a significant portion of the federal budget. These payments divert funds away from essential services and place an increasing burden on future generations.

Furthermore, wasteful spending creates a culture of complacency within government agencies. When inefficiencies go unaddressed, they become normalized, leading to a cycle of mismanagement that is difficult to break. This culture not only wastes resources but also diminishes the government's ability to address pressing issues effectively.

Conclusion and Transition
These case studies illustrate how wasteful spending permeates every level of government, affecting everything from national defense to local infrastructure. While some projects are laughable in their absurdity, others have serious consequences for taxpayers and the nation's fiscal health.

In the next chapter, we will explore how this waste directly impacts taxpayers, examining the financial burdens it creates and the opportunities lost due to mismanagement. By understanding the human and societal cost of wasteful spending, we can better appreciate the urgency of addressing this pervasive issue.

The direct and indirect costs of wasteful spending extend far beyond the government's balance sheets. Every taxpayer contributes a portion of their hard-earned income to fund public services and programs, but when those funds are mismanaged, it creates a cascading series of burdens that affect individuals, communities, and the nation as a whole. Wasteful spending is not just an issue of numbers—it has tangible consequences for the quality of life in the United States.

How Waste Affects the Taxpayer's Wallet
When government funds are wasted, the burden ultimately falls on taxpayers. This burden can manifest in various ways. First, there's the immediate financial impact: the more money wasted, the more revenue the government needs to raise through taxes or borrowing. For example, in 2022, the federal government's deficit exceeded $1 trillion, largely fueled by inefficient spending and a lack of fiscal discipline. This deficit spending contributes to the national debt, which taxpayers must eventually repay, either through higher taxes or reduced public services.

For families living paycheck to paycheck, the impact of wasteful spending is particularly acute. Higher taxes to cover budget shortfalls can mean less money for groceries, rent, or childcare. Similarly, reduced funding for essential services, such as public transportation or healthcare, forces individuals to pay out-of-pocket for what should be publicly funded. The cumulative effect is a heavier financial burden on the average American, with the poorest households often bearing the brunt of the impact.

Lost Opportunities for Public Services
Every dollar wasted is a dollar that could have been invested in vital services that directly benefit the public. For instance, the American Society of Civil Engineers (ASCE) estimates that the U.S. needs to invest $2.6 trillion over the next decade to repair and modernize its aging infrastructure. However, billions of dollars continue to be funneled into unnecessary or poorly managed projects instead.

Consider the $2 million spent on a marketing campaign for avocados or the $43 million gas station in Afghanistan. These funds could have been used to repair roads and bridges, improve public schools, or expand access to affordable housing. Instead, they were squandered, leaving critical needs unmet. The result is a nation where potholes go unfixed, classrooms remain overcrowded, and homelessness continues to rise—all while taxpayer dollars are spent on initiatives that provide little to no public benefit.

Erosion of Public Trust
Beyond the financial implications, wasteful spending undermines public trust in government. Taxpayers expect their contributions to be used responsibly and transparently, and when that expectation is not met, it fosters cynicism and disengagement. This erosion of trust has long-term consequences for democratic governance.

When citizens feel that their government is mismanaging resources, they are less likely to support new initiatives, even those that are well-planned and necessary. For example, proposals for increased infrastructure funding often face resistance, as voters question whether their money will be used effectively. This skepticism can delay or derail critical projects, further exacerbating existing problems.

The perception of government inefficiency also fuels political polarization. Wasteful spending becomes a rallying cry for critics, who use it to argue against public programs and advocate for smaller government. While fiscal responsibility is a legitimate concern, this politicization of wasteful spending often leads to gridlock, making it even harder to implement reforms or address pressing issues.

Long-Term Economic Consequences
At the macroeconomic level, wasteful spending contributes to the growing national debt, which poses significant risks for the nation's economic future. As of 2024, the U.S. national debt exceeds $33 trillion, with interest payments accounting for a substantial portion of the federal budget. These payments divert funds away from essential services and programs, creating a vicious cycle of borrowing and debt accumulation.

Moreover, high levels of debt can limit the government's ability to respond to future crises, such as economic recessions, natural disasters, or public health emergencies. When resources are tied up in servicing debt or covering the costs of past inefficiencies, there is less flexibility to address new challenges. This lack of preparedness puts the nation at greater risk and leaves taxpayers to shoulder the consequences.

The Emotional Toll on Citizens
Beyond the financial and structural impacts, wasteful spending also takes an emotional toll on citizens. For many, seeing their tax dollars wasted is not just frustrating—it's demoralizing. It creates a sense of powerlessness and alienation, as individuals feel they have little control over how their contributions are used. This emotional toll can lead to disengagement from civic life, with citizens becoming less likely to vote, participate in community initiatives, or advocate for change.

For example, when reports of wasteful spending make headlines, they often spark outrage on social media and in public forums. However, this outrage rarely translates into sustained action, as many citizens believe the problem is too deeply entrenched to fix. This sense of futility only exacerbates the issue, as a disengaged electorate is less likely to hold officials accountable for their actions.

Conclusion
The taxpayer's burden is more than just financial—it's a multifaceted issue that affects every aspect of civic life. Wasteful spending drains resources from critical services, increases the national debt, erodes public trust, and leaves citizens feeling disillusioned and powerless. These consequences underscore the urgent need for reform, not just to address individual cases of waste but to overhaul the systems and policies that allow inefficiencies to persist.

In the final page of this chapter, we will explore potential solutions to the problem of wasteful spending, focusing on strategies for improving accountability, efficiency, and transparency in government operations. By addressing these root causes, we can begin to alleviate the burden on taxpayers and restore confidence in public institutions.

The problem of wasteful government spending is not a new one, but addressing it requires more than outrage—it demands actionable solutions. With billions of taxpayer dollars at stake, it is crucial to implement reforms that prioritize accountability, efficiency, and transparency. By tackling the root causes of wasteful spending, we can reduce its impact, ensure public funds are used effectively, and restore trust in government institutions.

Improving Accountability
One of the most significant challenges in combating wasteful spending is the lack of accountability within government agencies. Programs often operate without clear benchmarks for success, making it difficult to evaluate their effectiveness. To address this, agencies must be required to establish measurable goals and report on their progress regularly. These reports should be made accessible to the public, allowing taxpayers to see where their money is going and how it is being used.

Additionally, independent oversight bodies, such as the Government Accountability Office (GAO) and the Office of Inspector General (OIG), play a critical role in identifying waste and recommending corrective actions. Strengthening these agencies by providing them with additional resources and authority can help ensure that their findings lead to meaningful changes. For example, when the GAO identifies inefficiencies in defense spending, the Department of Defense should be required to implement specific reforms and report on their outcomes.

Enhancing Efficiency

Efficiency is a cornerstone of responsible government spending. However, bureaucratic inefficiencies often lead to duplication of efforts and mismanagement of resources. To combat this, agencies should conduct regular audits to identify redundant programs and consolidate them where possible. For instance, if multiple agencies are tasked with similar responsibilities, such as environmental conservation or disaster response, their efforts should be coordinated to avoid overlap and reduce costs.

Embracing technology can also improve efficiency. Modernizing outdated systems and processes can streamline operations, reduce errors, and save money. For example, the Department of Veterans Affairs (VA) faced widespread criticism for its antiquated record-keeping system, which led to delays in processing benefits for veterans. By investing in a centralized, digital system, the VA was able to improve its operations and better serve its constituents.

Increasing Transparency

Transparency is essential for building public trust and ensuring that government spending aligns with taxpayer priorities. One way to achieve this is by making budget information more accessible and understandable. Agencies should be required to publish detailed breakdowns of their expenditures, along with explanations of how these funds contribute to their goals.

Citizen engagement tools, such as online dashboards, can also help increase transparency. These platforms allow taxpayers to track spending in real time, see how their contributions are being used, and provide feedback on government priorities. For example, some cities have implemented participatory budgeting programs, where residents can vote on how a portion of the budget is allocated. Expanding these initiatives to the federal level could give citizens a greater voice in decision-making and foster a sense of ownership over public funds.

Holding Officials Accountable
Wasteful spending often stems from political incentives that prioritize short-term gains over long-term benefits. Elected officials advocate for projects that benefit their constituents or political donors, even when those projects lack broader merit. To address this, stricter rules must be implemented to ensure that spending decisions are based on evidence and aligned with national priorities.

One potential solution is to introduce performance-based budgeting, where funding levels are tied to the outcomes of programs. If a program fails to meet its objectives, its budget could be reduced or reallocated to more effective initiatives. This approach incentivizes efficiency and ensures that taxpayer dollars are directed toward programs that deliver measurable results.

Whistleblower protections are another critical tool for combating waste. Employees within government agencies are often the first to notice inefficiencies or misconduct, but fear of retaliation can prevent them from speaking out. Strengthening protections for whistleblowers and providing anonymous reporting mechanisms can encourage employees to report waste without fear of reprisal.

Fostering a Culture of Responsibility
Ultimately, addressing wasteful spending requires a cultural shift within government. Agencies must move away from a mindset of "use it or lose it," where funds are spent simply to justify next year's budget. Instead, they should focus on achieving results and maximizing the impact of taxpayer dollars. Encouraging innovation, rewarding efficiency, and celebrating success stories can help foster a culture of responsibility and excellence.

Education and training programs for government employees can also play a role in reducing waste. By equipping employees with the skills and knowledge they need to manage resources effectively, agencies can minimize errors and improve their overall performance. For example, the Office of Management and Budget (OMB) could develop standardized training programs focused on budgeting, project management, and cost-benefit analysis.

Conclusion
Wasteful spending is a complex issue, but it is not insurmountable. By improving accountability, enhancing efficiency, increasing transparency, and holding officials accountable, we can begin to address the root causes of waste and ensure that taxpayer dollars are used effectively. These reforms require commitment and collaboration from all levels of government, as well as active participation from citizens.

As we move into the next chapter, we will explore how wasteful spending impacts taxpayers on a personal level, highlighting the financial and societal burdens it creates. Understanding these consequences is essential for building the momentum needed to drive meaningful change.

Chapter 2: The Taxpayer's Burden

The issue of wasteful government spending is often framed in terms of large numbers and abstract concepts. Trillions of dollars in national debt, billions in annual budget deficits, and millions wasted on individual projects are staggering figures, but what do they mean for the average taxpayer? To fully grasp the gravity of wasteful spending, it is essential to explore how it directly impacts citizens in tangible and often personal ways.

At its core, the taxpayer's burden represents the cost of inefficiency and mismanagement within government systems. Every dollar that is wasted on unnecessary projects, redundant programs, or poorly executed initiatives is a dollar that could have been used to improve public services, reduce the tax burden, or pay down the national debt. For the average American, this means higher taxes, fewer benefits, and diminished confidence in public institutions.

The Financial Impact on Families
To understand how wasteful spending affects taxpayers, consider the immediate financial burden it creates. Federal, state, and local governments rely on tax revenue to fund their operations. When funds are mismanaged or wasted, the shortfall must be addressed by raising taxes, increasing borrowing, or cutting essential services. None of these options are favorable for taxpayers.

Increased taxes, for instance, place a direct financial strain on households, especially those already living paycheck to paycheck. In 2022, the average American household paid approximately $10,500 in federal taxes. This figure does not include state and local taxes, which can add thousands more to the total. For families on tight budgets, even a small increase in tax rates can mean difficult choices, such as cutting back on groceries, delaying medical care, or forgoing educational opportunities.

Borrowing to cover budget deficits is another common approach, but it comes with its own set of consequences. The federal government's reliance on deficit spending has led to a national debt exceeding $33 trillion. Servicing this debt requires significant interest payments, which accounted for over $475 billion in 2023 alone.

These payments consume a growing share of the federal budget, leaving less room for programs that directly benefit taxpayers. Moreover, as interest rates rise, the cost of borrowing increases, further exacerbating the financial burden on future generations.

Lost Opportunities for Public Services

Perhaps the most significant consequence of wasteful spending is the opportunity cost it creates. Every dollar wasted on frivolous or redundant programs is a dollar that could have been invested in critical public services, such as education, healthcare, infrastructure, or public safety. These lost opportunities have a direct impact on the quality of life for millions of Americans.

Consider the state of the nation's infrastructure. According to the American Society of Civil Engineers (ASCE), the United States received a "C-" grade on its 2021 Infrastructure Report Card. Roads, bridges, water systems, and public transit networks across the country are in desperate need of repair and modernization. The ASCE estimates that addressing these issues will require an investment of $2.6 trillion over the next decade. However, billions of taxpayer dollars continue to be wasted on projects that provide little to no public benefit.

For example, a recent audit revealed that the Department of Transportation allocated $45 million for a highway expansion project in a sparsely populated rural area, despite clear evidence that the road was underused. Meanwhile, urban areas with heavy traffic congestion struggle to secure funding for necessary improvements. This misallocation of resources highlights how wasteful spending not only squanders taxpayer money but also perpetuates inequality in access to public services.

Healthcare is another area where wasteful spending has dire consequences. The United States spends more on healthcare per capita than any other country, yet millions of Americans remain uninsured or underinsured. Funds wasted on inefficient administrative processes, fraud, and redundant programs could be redirected to expand access to care, reduce medical costs, and improve health outcomes. For example, a recent investigation found that Medicare and Medicaid lose an estimated $60 billion annually to fraud and improper payments. Eliminating this waste could fund substantial improvements in these programs, benefiting millions of Americans.

Public Safety and Emergency Preparedness

Wasteful spending also affects the government's ability to respond to emergencies and ensure public safety. Natural disasters, public health crises, and national security threats require swift and effective action, but inefficiencies in government spending can hinder these efforts. For instance, during the COVID-19 pandemic, the federal government allocated billions of dollars in relief funds, but a lack of oversight led to widespread fraud and misuse. Reports estimate that up to $80 billion of pandemic relief funds were lost to fraudulent claims, including payments to fake businesses and duplicate applications.

These failures have real-world consequences. When funds are wasted, critical programs designed to support vulnerable populations during crises are underfunded, leaving individuals and communities without the resources they need. This not only exacerbates the immediate impact of the crisis but also undermines public confidence in the government's ability to manage resources effectively.

Conclusion and Transition

The taxpayer's burden is more than just a financial issue—it is a reflection of the government's priorities and the efficiency of its operations. Wasteful spending affects every aspect of society, from the quality of public services to the nation's ability to respond to emergencies. It erodes public trust, increases economic inequality, and places an unfair burden on current and future generations.

In the next section, we will delve deeper into specific examples of how wasteful spending impacts taxpayers, highlighting the human stories behind the numbers. By examining these cases, we can better understand the urgency of addressing this pervasive issue and the steps needed to create a more accountable and effective government.

The effects of wasteful government spending extend beyond dollar amounts—it impacts the everyday lives of citizens in ways that can be difficult to quantify but deeply felt. Each instance of inefficiency or misuse of funds creates ripple effects, diminishing the quality of life for millions of Americans. As we explore these impacts, it becomes clear that wasteful spending is not just a problem of mismanagement but a profound breach of trust between taxpayers and their government.

Education and the Opportunity Cost of Waste
One of the most glaring areas where wasteful spending exacts a toll is education. Across the country, schools face chronic underfunding, leading to overcrowded classrooms, outdated materials, and underpaid teachers. Meanwhile, billions of dollars are allocated annually to projects that offer no tangible benefit to students or the education system at large.

For instance, in recent years, millions were spent on a federally funded program designed to promote the use of tablet computers in schools without a clear implementation plan. While the idea of integrating technology into classrooms is commendable, the lack of training for teachers and infrastructure to support the initiative resulted in the devices going largely unused. This misstep left schools without the resources they truly needed, such as basic supplies, extracurricular programs, and professional development opportunities for educators.

This type of waste highlights the opportunity cost of poor spending decisions. Instead of addressing systemic issues, funds are diverted to projects that fail to make a meaningful impact. For students, this translates to fewer learning opportunities and diminished prospects for success in an increasingly competitive world.

Healthcare: A System Under Pressure
Healthcare is another sector where the effects of wasteful spending are deeply felt. Despite the United States spending more on healthcare per capita than any other nation, many Americans struggle to access affordable care. Administrative inefficiencies, fraud, and redundant programs contribute to the problem, diverting resources away from patient care and innovation.

For example, the improper payments made by Medicare and Medicaid, estimated at $60 billion annually, represent a significant drain on resources. These payments often result from billing errors, fraud, or inadequate oversight. While these issues may seem like bureaucratic glitches, they have real-world consequences for patients who rely on these programs for life-saving treatments and medications.

Imagine the impact of redirecting even a fraction of these wasted funds toward expanding access to preventive care or subsidizing prescription drugs. By reducing waste, the healthcare system could serve more people and deliver better outcomes, alleviating the financial burden on both taxpayers and patients.

Infrastructure: Paying the Price of Neglect

The nation's crumbling infrastructure is perhaps the most visible consequence of misallocated resources. From pothole-ridden roads to aging bridges, the state of public infrastructure affects every American in some way. Yet, year after year, funds that could address these critical needs are squandered on less pressing or poorly executed projects.

One striking example is the $25 million spent on a pedestrian bridge in a rural area that sees fewer than 50 walkers per day. While the intention to improve safety was noble, the project's cost far exceeded its practical benefits, especially when contrasted with the pressing need to repair major highways and urban transit systems serving millions.

The American Society of Civil Engineers (ASCE) estimates that subpar infrastructure costs the average household $3,300 annually in delays, vehicle repairs, and other indirect expenses. These hidden costs compound the taxpayer's burden, making wasteful spending an issue that directly impacts household budgets.

The Emotional and Psychological Impact

Beyond financial and structural consequences, wasteful spending also takes an emotional toll on citizens. For many, the knowledge that their hard-earned money is being misused creates a sense of frustration and powerlessness. This emotional response is not just about dollars wasted—it's about the broken promises and unfulfilled potential that wasteful spending represents.

Consider the psychological impact of living in a community where public services are underfunded. Parents worry about the quality of education their children receive. Patients struggle to navigate a healthcare system that seems designed to frustrate rather than help. Commuters grow weary of navigating roads and transit systems in disrepair. These daily struggles compound, creating a pervasive sense of dissatisfaction and distrust in government institutions.

The Impact on Future Generations

One of the most concerning aspects of wasteful spending is its long-term impact on future generations. The growing national debt, fueled in part by inefficiencies and mismanagement, represents a financial burden that today's youth will be forced to bear. As interest payments consume an increasing share of the federal budget, fewer resources will be available for investments in education, healthcare, and infrastructure—programs that are critical for ensuring a prosperous future.

For young Americans, this translates to higher taxes, reduced economic opportunities, and an uncertain future. The compounding effects of wasteful spending today will ripple through the economy for decades, shaping the lives of generations to come.

Conclusion and Transition

The taxpayer's burden is not just about financial costs—it is about missed opportunities, diminished quality of life, and a growing sense of disillusionment with public institutions. Wasteful spending affects every aspect of society, from the quality of public services to the nation's ability to invest in its future.

In the next page, we will examine the human stories behind these impacts, exploring how individuals and families experience the consequences of wasteful government spending in their daily lives. By connecting the broader issue to personal experiences, we can better understand the urgency of addressing this pervasive problem.

When examining wasteful government spending, it's easy to get lost in numbers and figures. Billions of dollars misallocated here, millions improperly spent there—these sums are staggering but abstract. However, behind every misused dollar is a human story. The consequences of these inefficiencies are felt most acutely by individuals, families, and communities across the country. By exploring these personal impacts, the scale of wasteful spending becomes not just a fiscal issue but a deeply personal one.

Families Struggling Under the Weight of Inefficiency
Consider the plight of families in low-income communities who depend on public programs to meet their basic needs. These families pay taxes, often sacrificing necessities to do so, in the hope that public services will improve their quality of life. Yet, when these funds are mismanaged, the programs designed to support them fail to deliver.

Take, for example, public housing projects. Federal and state agencies allocate billions annually to maintain and develop affordable housing. However, wasteful spending often results in funds being funneled into poorly planned or mismanaged projects. A 2021 report revealed that a housing authority in a major U.S. city spent $2 million on consultants for a redevelopment project that never materialized. Meanwhile, thousands of families remained on waiting lists, struggling to find safe and affordable places to live.

For these families, the consequences are dire. Children grow up in unstable housing environments, affecting their education and mental health. Parents face constant stress, juggling rent payments with other expenses. This cycle of insecurity perpetuates poverty, undermining the very purpose of the programs intended to help.

Small Businesses Hit by Mismanagement
Wasteful spending also affects small businesses, the backbone of the American economy. Small business owners rely on government programs for support, whether through grants, loans, or infrastructure investments that improve the environment in which they operate. However, when these programs are mismanaged, entrepreneurs bear the brunt of the consequences.

During the COVID-19 pandemic, the federal government introduced the Paycheck Protection Program (PPP) to provide financial relief to small businesses. While the program's intentions were noble, its execution was riddled with inefficiencies and fraud. Reports estimate that up to $80 billion in PPP funds were fraudulently claimed, often by fake businesses or large corporations that found loopholes in the system.

For legitimate small business owners, this waste represented missed opportunities. Many were unable to secure the funds they needed to stay afloat, leading to closures and layoffs. The loss of these businesses not only affected the owners but also their employees, customers, and communities, illustrating the far-reaching impact of government inefficiency.

Communities Left Behind
Entire communities suffer when wasteful spending diverts resources from essential services. Public infrastructure, for instance, is a cornerstone of community development, enabling residents to travel safely, access clean water, and enjoy recreational spaces. Yet, year after year, funds intended for these purposes are squandered on poorly executed projects.

In one notable case, a city in the Midwest allocated $6.5 million to revamp its public park system. While the initial plans promised upgraded facilities and improved accessibility, mismanagement led to delays, cost overruns, and ultimately an incomplete project. Meanwhile, residents were left with deteriorating parks and playgrounds, unable to enjoy the benefits of their tax dollars.

These failures are not just inconvenient—they can have long-term consequences for community well-being. Poor infrastructure discourages investment, hampers economic growth, and reduces property values. It also erodes residents' trust in local government, making it harder to rally support for future initiatives.

The Emotional Toll on Taxpayers
Beyond the tangible effects, wasteful spending takes an emotional toll on taxpayers. For many, the knowledge that their hard-earned money is being wasted is a source of frustration and anger. This

emotional burden is compounded by the sense of powerlessness many feel when faced with a system that seems resistant to
change.

Consider a middle-class family working to save for their child's college education. Every year, they pay thousands of dollars in taxes,
believing that these funds will contribute to a better future for their
community and country. Yet, when they see headlines about frivolous expenditures—such as the $2 million spent on a study examin-
ing shrimp on treadmills—it's hard not to feel disillusioned.

This disillusionment can lead to disengagement from civic life.
Taxpayers who lose faith in the government's ability to manage
resources responsibly are less likely to vote, participate in public
discussions, or advocate for change. This creates a vicious cycle
in which inefficiency goes unchallenged, further perpetuating the
problem.

Generational Inequity
Perhaps the most troubling aspect of wasteful spending is its impact on future generations. The growing national debt, fueled by inefficiencies and mismanagement, represents a financial burden that
today's youth will inherit. As interest payments consume an increasing share of the federal budget, fewer resources will be available for
investments in education, healthcare, and innovation—areas critical
for ensuring a prosperous future.

Young Americans already face significant challenges, from student
loan debt to a competitive job market. Adding the burden of a mismanaged economy only exacerbates these issues, limiting opportunities and creating an uncertain future. For many, the knowledge
that they will bear the cost of today's inefficiencies adds a layer of
anxiety to an already challenging reality.

Conclusion and Transition
The personal stories behind wasteful spending reveal the human
cost of inefficiency. From struggling families and small business
owners to entire communities left behind, the consequences of
mismanagement extend far beyond financial losses. These stories
underscore the urgency of addressing wasteful spending, not just

to save money but to restore faith in public institutions and create a better future for all Americans.

In the next section, we will explore how wasteful spending contributes to systemic inequality, perpetuating disparities in access to resources and opportunities. By examining these broader societal impacts, we can better understand the full scope of the taxpayer's burden and the need for meaningful reform.

Wasteful spending not only drains financial resources but also exacerbates systemic inequality, deepening the divide between those who can afford inefficiencies and those who cannot. By mismanaging public funds, the government inadvertently perpetuates disparities in access to essential services, opportunities, and infrastructure. These inequalities disproportionately impact marginalized communities, amplifying the challenges they face and hindering efforts to achieve a more equitable society.

The Role of Wasteful Spending in Education Disparities
Education is often referred to as the great equalizer, but wasteful spending undermines its potential to level the playing field. Schools in affluent areas typically have access to better resources, more experienced teachers, and state-of-the-art facilities, while schools in low-income communities struggle to provide even the basics. When funds are mismanaged, the disparities only grow.

A particularly glaring example of this is the allocation of federal education funds to initiatives with limited practical value. One such instance involved a multimillion-dollar program aimed at studying the long-term effects of technology use in classrooms. While the idea was well-intentioned, poor execution meant that the funds were largely spent on administrative costs and pilot programs that never scaled. Meanwhile, schools in underprivileged districts continued to operate with outdated textbooks, insufficient technology, and overcrowded classrooms.

These inefficiencies widen the education gap, leaving students in low-income areas at a significant disadvantage. Without equitable access to quality education, these students are less likely to attend college or secure high-paying jobs, perpetuating cycles of poverty and inequality.

Infrastructure and Geographic Inequality

Infrastructure is another area where wasteful spending contributes to inequality. Urban and rural areas often experience vastly different levels of investment, with wealthier regions benefiting from well-maintained roads, reliable public transit, and modern utilities, while poorer areas are left with crumbling infrastructure and inadequate services.

For instance, billions of dollars have been allocated to transportation projects in major metropolitan areas that already have robust transit systems. While these investments can be justified in terms of economic growth, they often come at the expense of rural or economically disadvantaged regions. In one case, a rural highway project that would have improved access to healthcare and education for thousands of residents was delayed for years due to funding shortages—shortages caused, in part, by mismanagement of federal transportation grants.

This imbalance not only limits opportunities for residents of underserved areas but also creates a feedback loop in which lack of investment leads to stagnation and further neglect. Communities without adequate infrastructure struggle to attract businesses, improve property values, or provide residents with the resources they need to thrive.

Healthcare Inequities Amplified by Waste

Healthcare inequities in the United States are well-documented, with factors such as income, race, and geography playing significant roles in determining access to care. Wasteful spending within the healthcare system exacerbates these disparities, diverting resources away from the populations that need them most.

For example, the improper allocation of Medicaid funds often results in wealthier states receiving a disproportionate share of resources, while poorer states struggle to meet the needs of their residents. Fraudulent claims and administrative inefficiencies further deplete already limited funds, reducing the availability of services for low-income families and rural communities.

One study found that fraudulent billing practices in Medicaid cost taxpayers an estimated $36 billion annually. These funds could have been used to expand access to preventive care, reduce wait times for critical treatments, or address shortages of healthcare providers in underserved areas. Instead, they were lost to inefficiencies, leaving vulnerable populations to bear the brunt of the consequences.

Economic Inequality and the Cost of Mismanagement
Economic inequality is both a cause and a consequence of wasteful spending. When public funds are mismanaged, they often fail to reach the people and programs that need them most, reinforcing existing disparities. This is particularly evident in economic development initiatives, which are frequently criticized for favoring large corporations over small businesses and local communities.

One striking example involved a federal program designed to stimulate job growth in economically depressed areas. While the program successfully attracted several major corporations to participate, it was later revealed that the majority of the funds were spent on tax incentives and subsidies for companies that did not deliver on their promises. Meanwhile, local small businesses—the backbone of these communities—received little to no support, despite their potential to create sustainable, long-term economic growth.

This pattern of favoring the powerful over the vulnerable perpetuates cycles of inequality. Communities that could benefit most from economic development programs are often left behind, while wealthier areas and large corporations continue to thrive.

The Psychological Toll of Inequality
The emotional and psychological effects of inequality created by wasteful spending are profound. For individuals in underserved communities, the knowledge that their tax dollars are being misused adds to the frustration of living without adequate resources. It creates a sense of injustice and hopelessness, as people feel powerless to change a system that seems designed to fail them.

This emotional toll is compounded by the perception that the gov-

ernment prioritizes the interests of the wealthy and well-connect-
ed over those of ordinary citizens. When taxpayers see billions of
dollars spent on corporate subsidies or redundant projects while
their communities lack basic services, it erodes their faith in public
institutions and fosters resentment.

Conclusion and Transition
Wasteful spending not only wastes money—it deepens societal
divides and perpetuates inequality. By mismanaging resources, the
government fails to address the needs of its most vulnerable citizens, widening gaps in education, healthcare, and economic opportunity. These failures have lasting consequences, both for individuals and for the nation as a whole.

In the next page, we will explore potential solutions to the problem of wasteful spending, focusing on strategies to promote equity
and ensure that taxpayer dollars are used to benefit all Americans.
These solutions represent a path forward, one that prioritizes efficiency, accountability, and fairness in public spending.

Addressing the taxpayer's burden requires more than identifying
instances of waste—it demands systemic change that promotes
equity, efficiency, and accountability in public spending. While the
challenges are significant, there are actionable solutions that can
alleviate the burden on taxpayers and ensure government funds
are used effectively. These reforms must target the root causes of
wasteful spending, prioritize the needs of underserved communities, and foster trust in public institutions.

Promoting Equity in Public Spending
One of the most critical steps in addressing wasteful spending is
ensuring that resources are allocated equitably. This means prioritizing investments in underserved communities and addressing
systemic disparities in access to education, healthcare, and infrastructure.

A potential solution is the implementation of targeted funding programs that focus on measurable outcomes for marginalized populations. For example, rather than providing blanket subsidies to entire
industries, funding could be directed toward specific initiatives that

benefit low-income families, such as expanding access to affordable childcare or creating job training programs in economically depressed areas. By tying funds to clearly defined goals, policymakers can ensure that public spending addresses real needs and reduces inequality.

Enhancing Oversight and Accountability
Effective oversight is essential to preventing waste and ensuring taxpayer dollars are spent wisely. This requires robust monitoring mechanisms that can identify inefficiencies and hold decision-makers accountable for mismanagement. Independent oversight agencies, such as the Government Accountability Office (GAO), play a crucial role in this process, but they must be empowered with the resources and authority needed to enforce their recommendations.

For example, creating a centralized database to track government expenditures in real-time could improve transparency and allow for more effective oversight. This database could be accessible to both policymakers and the public, enabling citizens to monitor how their tax dollars are being used and raise concerns about potential misuse.

Additionally, whistleblower protections must be strengthened to encourage government employees to report instances of fraud or inefficiency. Fear of retaliation often prevents individuals from speaking out, allowing wasteful practices to continue unchecked. By safeguarding whistleblowers and providing anonymous reporting mechanisms, the government can create a culture of accountability that deters waste.

Investing in Modernization
Outdated systems and processes are a significant source of inefficiency in government operations. Investing in modernization can help streamline workflows, reduce errors, and improve the overall effectiveness of public programs. For instance, many government agencies still rely on manual processes or antiquated software for tasks such as record-keeping and financial management. Upgrading these systems can save time and money while reducing the risk of fraud and mismanagement.

One area where modernization has shown promise is healthcare. The adoption of electronic health records (EHRs) has improved efficiency and patient care in many hospitals and clinics, allowing providers to access accurate, up-to-date information quickly. Similar innovations could be applied to other sectors, such as education and transportation, to improve service delivery and reduce waste.

Engaging Citizens in Budgeting Decisions
Citizen engagement is a powerful tool for promoting accountability and ensuring public funds are used to address community needs. Participatory budgeting programs, which allow residents to have a direct say in how a portion of the budget is allocated, have proven successful in cities across the United States and around the world. These programs empower citizens to identify priorities, propose projects, and vote on how funds should be spent.

Expanding participatory budgeting to the federal level could increase transparency and trust in government spending. By involving taxpayers in the decision-making process, policymakers can better align expenditures with public needs and priorities, reducing the risk of waste and inefficiency.

Addressing the National Debt
Finally, any effort to reduce the taxpayer's burden must address the growing national debt. While reducing wasteful spending is an important first step, long-term fiscal sustainability requires a comprehensive approach that includes both spending reforms and revenue enhancements. This could involve reevaluating tax policies to ensure they are fair and effective, as well as prioritizing investments that generate economic growth and improve quality of life.

For example, investing in education and workforce development has been shown to yield significant returns by increasing productivity and earning potential. Similarly, infrastructure improvements can stimulate economic activity, creating jobs and attracting businesses to underserved areas. By focusing on high-impact investments, the government can reduce the deficit over time while improving outcomes for taxpayers.

Restoring Public Trust

Ultimately, addressing wasteful spending is about more than saving money—it's about restoring trust in public institutions and demonstrating that the government is capable of managing resources responsibly. This requires a commitment to transparency, accountability, and equity in every aspect of public spending. When taxpayers see that their contributions are being used effectively to improve society, they are more likely to support government initiatives and participate in civic life.

Restoring trust also means acknowledging past failures and taking concrete steps to prevent them from recurring. By learning from mistakes and implementing meaningful reforms, policymakers can rebuild confidence in the government's ability to serve the public good.

Conclusion
The taxpayer's burden is a complex issue that requires a multifaceted solution. By promoting equity, enhancing oversight, investing in modernization, engaging citizens, and addressing the national debt, the government can reduce wasteful spending and ensure taxpayer dollars are used to benefit all Americans. These reforms are not just about balancing the budget—they are about creating a fairer, more efficient, and more accountable system that works for everyone.

In the next chapter, we will delve into specific examples of wasteful spending that highlight the absurdity and scale of the problem. From funding shrimp on treadmills to building gas stations in conflict zones, these cases underscore the urgent need for reform and the potential for meaningful change.

Chapter 3: Absurd Projects and Grants

Wasteful government spending takes many forms, but some examples stand out for their sheer absurdity. These projects, often ridiculed in media headlines, illustrate the extremes of mismanagement and highlight the need for greater oversight and accountability. From funding obscure research to financing questionable international programs, these cases not only waste taxpayer money but also undermine public trust in government institutions.

The $592,000 Shrimp Treadmill Study
Few examples of wasteful spending have garnered as much public attention as the infamous shrimp treadmill study. Funded by the National Science Foundation (NSF), this $592,000 research project sought to examine how shrimp responded to exercise on tiny underwater treadmills. While proponents of the study argued that it contributed to our understanding of marine biology and environmental stressors, critics questioned the practicality and necessity of such a niche experiment.

The shrimp treadmill study became a symbol of frivolous spending, sparking debates about the criteria used to approve research grants. Although scientific inquiry is essential, projects like this raise important questions about the prioritization of funding. Could these resources have been better spent on pressing issues, such as improving public education, advancing medical research, or addressing climate change? The case highlights the need for clearer guidelines and stricter evaluations of grant proposals to ensure taxpayer dollars are used effectively.

The $2.5 Million Bug Buffet
Another eyebrow-raising example comes from a $2.5 million federal grant allocated to study whether Americans would eat insects as a sustainable protein source. The project aimed to explore alternative food options in response to concerns about climate change and food security. While the concept of edible insects is gaining traction globally, the grant's execution and outcomes were met with skepticism.

Critics argued that the research duplicated existing studies and offered little new insight. Additionally, many questioned whether taxpayer funds should be used to promote a practice that is still culturally taboo for many Americans. The project's defenders maintained that it addressed an important issue, but the lack of measurable impact made it a prime target for criticism.

This example underscores a common theme in wasteful spending: the allocation of funds to projects with limited practical applications or unclear benefits. While innovation is vital, it must be balanced with accountability and a focus on delivering tangible results.

The $43 Million Gas Station in Afghanistan

Wasteful spending is not confined to domestic projects—it extends to international programs as well. One of the most egregious examples is the $43 million spent on building a single gas station in Afghanistan. The project, funded by the Department of Defense, was intended to promote the use of compressed natural gas (CNG) as a cleaner and more cost-effective alternative to traditional fuels.

However, the gas station's construction and operation were plagued by mismanagement and inefficiency. The costs far exceeded initial estimates, and the project ultimately failed to achieve its objectives. Reports revealed that there was little demand for CNG in the region, and the necessary infrastructure to support its use was lacking. Furthermore, the project lacked proper oversight, allowing costs to spiral out of control.

The Afghanistan gas station debacle serves as a cautionary tale about the risks of undertaking large-scale projects without thorough planning and evaluation. It also highlights the importance of aligning foreign aid initiatives with the needs and capabilities of the target population.

Butterflies in Europe: A $1 Million Question

In another puzzling case, the federal government allocated $1 million to study the migration patterns of European butterflies. While understanding biodiversity is important, critics questioned why American taxpayers were funding research that seemed to have little relevance to the United States. The grant raised concerns about the prioritization of international research projects and the criteria used to determine their funding.

This example illustrates the need for greater scrutiny of grants that focus on topics outside the scope of national priorities. While global collaboration is valuable, it must be weighed against the immediate needs of American taxpayers, particularly in areas such as healthcare, education, and infrastructure.

Conclusion and Transition

These examples of absurd projects and grants are more than just fodder for headlines—they represent systemic issues in the allocation and oversight of public funds. Each case underscores the need for stricter guidelines, more rigorous evaluations, and increased accountability in government spending. By addressing these shortcomings, we can reduce waste, restore public trust, and ensure that taxpayer dollars are used to address pressing societal needs.

In the next section, we will delve into more examples of wasteful spending, focusing on how inefficiencies in defense, healthcare, and education exacerbate the problem. These cases further highlight the importance of reform and the potential for meaningful change.

The absurdity of some government projects highlights not just the misuse of funds but also the systemic flaws in planning, oversight, and execution. While some initiatives fail because of a lack of relevance or practicality, others falter due to poor management, misaligned priorities, or unchecked costs. Defense spending, a cornerstone of the federal budget, is rife with examples of waste that illustrate how even critical areas are vulnerable to inefficiency.

The $640 Toilet Seat

Few examples of wasteful spending are as infamous as the Department of Defense's $640 toilet seat. First exposed in the 1980s, this case became a symbol of Pentagon overspending and inefficiency. The exorbitant cost was attributed to bureaucratic procurement processes, which involved multiple layers of approvals, specifications, and contractors. While the military defended the expense by citing the unique requirements of the aircraft it was designed for, public outcry over such a seemingly trivial item fueled demands for greater accountability.

Decades later, the toilet seat remains a cautionary tale about the dangers of unchecked spending in defense contracts. The lesson is clear: even small oversights in procurement processes can lead to significant waste when multiplied across the vast scope of military operations.

$1.3 Billion on Planes That Were Never Used

In another striking example of defense waste, the Pentagon spent $1.3 billion on C-27J Spartan aircraft, only to mothball them shortly after acquisition. The planes were intended for use by the Air National Guard but were deemed unnecessary due to changing mission requirements. Instead of being deployed, the aircraft were stored in the Arizona desert, where they remain unused to this day.

This case highlights a critical flaw in defense planning: the failure to adapt procurement decisions to evolving needs. While the original purchase may have been justified, the inability to repurpose or resell the planes represents a significant loss of taxpayer money. It also underscores the importance of conducting thorough cost-benefit analyses before committing to large-scale purchases.

$36 Million on an Unused Military Facility

The U.S. military has also been criticized for spending $36 million on the construction of a state-of-the-art command and control facility in Afghanistan that was never used. The building, which included offices, conference rooms, and high-tech equipment, was completed in 2013 but was abandoned shortly thereafter due to changes in operational strategy. Reports revealed that military officials had raised concerns about the project's necessity during its planning stages, but construction proceeded regardless.

The facility's abandonment drew sharp criticism from watchdog groups and lawmakers, who argued that it exemplified the broader issue of wasteful spending in military operations. While the Department of Defense acknowledged the mistake, the incident underscored the need for more stringent oversight of overseas projects and a greater emphasis on flexibility in planning.

Overpriced Spare Parts and Inventory Waste
The Pentagon's inventory management system has long been a source of inefficiency and waste. One notorious example involved the purchase of spare helicopter parts at inflated prices, with some items marked up by as much as 1,000%. In one case, the military paid $8,000 for a helicopter part that cost only $500 on the open market. These overpayments were attributed to poor oversight and a lack of competition among contractors.

In addition to overpriced parts, the Department of Defense has been criticized for stockpiling billions of dollars' worth of unused inventory. A 2016 report revealed that the Pentagon had accumulated over $14 billion in excess equipment and supplies, much of which was sitting unused in warehouses. This surplus represents a significant waste of resources, particularly when defense budgets continue to face scrutiny.

Lessons from Defense Waste
These examples from the defense sector illustrate the systemic issues that contribute to wasteful spending. While defense is a critical component of national security, its vast budget and complex operations make it particularly susceptible to inefficiency. Addressing these issues requires reforms at multiple levels, including:

Streamlining Procurement Processes: Simplifying the procedures for purchasing equipment and supplies can reduce costs and minimize the risk of overpayments.
Enhancing Oversight: Independent audits and stricter controls can help ensure that funds are used effectively and align with strategic priorities.
Improving Inventory Management: Implementing modern logistics systems can help prevent overstocking and ensure that resources are allocated where they are needed most.

Conclusion and Transition
The waste in defense spending is a microcosm of the broader issues facing government operations. These examples reveal how systemic inefficiencies, poor planning, and a lack of accountability

can lead to staggering losses, even in areas as critical as national security. While some progress has been made in addressing these challenges, much work remains to be done.

In the next section, we will examine wasteful spending in other sectors, including education, healthcare, and public infrastructure. By exploring these areas, we can gain a deeper understanding of the scope of the problem and the urgent need for meaningful reform.

While defense spending often captures headlines for its scale, wasteful spending is not confined to the military. Education, healthcare, and public infrastructure are also riddled with inefficiencies and mismanagement, which not only waste taxpayer dollars but also directly harm the public by diverting resources from essential services. These examples show how deeply wasteful spending permeates every level of government.

The $1 Billion Failed Virtual School Initiative

Education is a cornerstone of a nation's future, and government spending in this area is meant to prepare the next generation for success. However, not all education initiatives achieve their intended goals. One striking example is the federal government's investment in a $1 billion virtual school program designed to increase access to online learning in underserved communities.

The program was plagued by poor execution and lack of oversight from the start. Many schools lacked the necessary infrastructure to implement virtual learning effectively, and teachers received little to no training on how to use the new platforms. As a result, student engagement and academic outcomes fell short of expectations. In some cases, the online systems were so poorly designed that students could not access their coursework at all.

Critics argued that the funds could have been better spent addressing the root causes of educational inequity, such as providing resources for struggling schools or raising teacher salaries. Instead, the failed initiative became another example of how ambitious projects can falter without proper planning and accountability.

$10 Million in Improper Medicaid Payments

Healthcare spending is one of the largest components of the federal budget, and programs like Medicaid are vital for ensuring access to care for low-income Americans. However, inefficiencies and fraud within these programs lead to billions of dollars in waste each year.

One investigation revealed that a state Medicaid program issued $10 million in improper payments to ineligible recipients. These payments were made due to errors in the eligibility verification process, which failed to identify individuals who no longer qualified for benefits. While the intent of Medicaid is to provide a safety net for vulnerable populations, such errors undermine the program's effectiveness and erode public confidence in its management.

Efforts to recover the funds were hampered by bureaucratic delays and resistance from local agencies, further highlighting the need for stronger oversight and enforcement mechanisms. These missteps not only waste taxpayer money but also divert resources from those who genuinely need assistance.

The $200,000 Staircase

Infrastructure projects are often touted as investments in public welfare, but poor planning and execution can turn them into costly mistakes. A case in point is the $200,000 outdoor staircase constructed in a public park in a major U.S. city. While the staircase was intended to improve accessibility and safety, its exorbitant cost sparked outrage among taxpayers and urban planners alike.

Critics pointed out that a local contractor had offered to build a similar structure for less than $30,000, but city officials chose a more expensive design without providing a clear justification. The staircase quickly became a symbol of government inefficiency, with taxpayers questioning why their money was being spent so recklessly on a relatively minor project.

This example underscores the importance of transparency and competition in public works projects. By soliciting multiple bids and thoroughly evaluating cost-benefit analyses, governments can avoid overspending on basic infrastructure.

$3.4 Million to Study the Behavior of Drunken Birds

Research grants, while often essential for scientific advancement, sometimes draw criticism for their seemingly frivolous focus. One such grant allocated $3.4 million to study the effects of alcohol consumption on birds. The researchers aimed to understand how drunken behavior in birds could provide insights into human decision-making and social interactions.

While the study's defenders argued that it contributed to behavioral science, its practical applications were not immediately clear to the public. Critics questioned whether the project justified its hefty price tag, particularly when other areas of research—such as cancer treatments or renewable energy—are underfunded.

This case highlights the need for stricter criteria when approving research grants. While innovation often comes from unexpected places, the allocation of public funds must be guided by a clear understanding of the potential benefits and relevance to taxpayer priorities.

Public Transportation Debacles

Public transportation is a critical service that connects communities and reduces traffic congestion, yet it is often plagued by wasteful spending. A particularly glaring example occurred in a major metropolitan area, where a $2.2 billion subway expansion project ran billions over budget and years behind schedule. Mismanagement, poor contractor oversight, and design changes during construction contributed to the delays and cost overruns.

In the meantime, commuters continued to face overcrowded trains, outdated infrastructure, and unreliable service. The project's failures not only wasted taxpayer money but also delayed much-needed improvements to the city's transit system, leaving residents frustrated and underserved.

Conclusion and Transition

The examples from education, healthcare, infrastructure, and research show how wasteful spending extends far beyond defense. These failures are not just about lost dollars—they represent lost opportunities to address pressing societal challenges and improve the quality of life for all Americans.

In the next section, we will explore the systemic factors that allow such inefficiencies to persist, from bureaucratic inertia to political incentives. By understanding these root causes, we can begin to identify meaningful solutions that reduce waste and restore trust in government spending.

The sheer volume of wasteful spending in government reveals a troubling pattern: systemic inefficiencies and misaligned priorities often take precedence over fiscal responsibility. From extravagant public works projects to poorly conceived research grants, these examples underscore the need for fundamental reforms. However, understanding the root causes of such waste is crucial for addressing it effectively.

The Role of Bureaucratic Inertia

Bureaucratic inertia is a significant factor behind wasteful spending. Government agencies often operate under rigid rules and outdated processes, making it difficult to adapt to changing circumstances or prioritize efficiency. Once a program is established, it can persist for years—sometimes decades—without proper evaluation of its relevance or effectiveness.

Take, for instance, the numerous redundant programs across federal agencies. A Government Accountability Office (GAO) report identified dozens of instances where multiple departments were tasked with similar objectives, such as workforce training or small business assistance. These overlapping responsibilities not only waste money but also create confusion and inefficiency in service delivery. Consolidating such programs could save billions of dollars annually, yet political and bureaucratic resistance often prevents meaningful change.

Political Incentives and Misaligned Priorities

Political incentives play a major role in perpetuating wasteful spending. Elected officials frequently advocate for projects that benefit their constituencies or align with their political agendas, even if those projects lack broader merit. This practice, known as pork-barrel spending, diverts resources from critical national priorities to localized initiatives with limited impact.

One illustrative example is the allocation of millions of dollars for decorative pedestrian bridges in small towns while urban centers struggle to fund basic infrastructure repairs. While these projects may serve as tangible achievements for politicians to showcase during reelection campaigns, they often fail to address pressing societal needs, such as affordable housing or public transit improvements.

Similarly, political considerations often lead to the funding of unnecessary defense contracts or agricultural subsidies, benefiting powerful interest groups at the expense of taxpayers. These expenditures highlight the need for mechanisms that prioritize long-term national interests over short-term political gains.

Lack of Oversight and Transparency

A lack of oversight is another critical driver of wasteful spending. Many government programs operate with minimal accountability, allowing inefficiencies to persist unchecked. In some cases, funds are allocated to projects without clear benchmarks for success or mechanisms for evaluating their outcomes.

For example, federal disaster relief programs have been criticized for allocating billions of dollars with little oversight, resulting in waste and fraud. While rapid response is essential during emergencies, the absence of proper controls has led to instances where funds were misused or diverted to unrelated projects. Strengthening oversight and requiring detailed reporting could help prevent such misuse and ensure that resources are directed where they are needed most.

Transparency is equally important in combating waste. Taxpayers have a right to know how their money is being spent, yet many government expenditures remain shrouded in opacity. By making detailed budget information publicly accessible and easy to understand, policymakers can empower citizens to hold their representatives accountable for wasteful spending.

The Impact of Cultural Norms

A less tangible but equally important factor is the culture within government agencies. In many cases, there is an unspoken expectation to "spend it or lose it." This mentality encourages agencies to exhaust their budgets, even on unnecessary expenses, to ensure they receive the same level of funding in future years. Such practices not only waste resources but also discourage innovation and efficiency.

Changing this culture requires a shift in how success is measured. Instead of focusing solely on spending levels, agencies should be evaluated based on outcomes and efficiency. Recognizing and rewarding cost-saving measures can incentivize officials to prioritize fiscal responsibility without compromising the quality of services.

Moving Toward Solutions

The examples of wasteful spending discussed throughout this chapter highlight systemic issues that require comprehensive solutions. Key strategies include:

Strengthening Oversight: Expanding the authority and resources of watchdog agencies like the GAO can help identify inefficiencies and hold officials accountable.
Enhancing Transparency: Public access to detailed budget information can empower citizens to advocate for better spending practices.
Reforming Procurement Processes: Simplifying and modernizing procurement rules can reduce costs and improve efficiency in government contracts.
Prioritizing Results: Shifting the focus from spending levels to measurable outcomes can encourage agencies to use resources more effectively.
Encouraging Citizen Engagement: Programs like participatory budgeting allow taxpayers to have a direct say in how public funds are allocated, fostering accountability and trust.

Conclusion

The absurd projects and grants explored in this chapter are symptoms of a larger problem: a government system that often prioritizes inertia, political considerations, and outdated practices over accountability and efficiency. Addressing these issues requires a commitment to systemic reform, guided by the principles of transparency, oversight, and fiscal responsibility.

In the next chapter, we will delve into widespread bureaucratic inefficiencies that contribute to wasteful spending. From overlapping responsibilities to outdated systems, these inefficiencies represent both a challenge and an opportunity for meaningful change.

Chapter 4: Widespread Bureaucratic Inefficiencies

Government wasteful spending is often rooted in systemic inefficiencies embedded within bureaucratic structures. These inefficiencies range from overlapping agency responsibilities to outdated processes and a lack of technological modernization. Together, they create an environment where mismanagement flourishes, making it difficult to maximize the value of taxpayer dollars. To address wasteful spending effectively, it is essential to understand the root causes of bureaucratic inefficiencies and explore strategies for reform.

Overlapping Responsibilities Across Agencies

One of the most significant contributors to inefficiency in government spending is the duplication of responsibilities across multiple agencies. A prime example is workforce development programs. A report by the Government Accountability Office (GAO) found that 47 separate federal programs across nine agencies were tasked with providing employment and training services. Despite their shared mission, these programs often operated independently, leading to redundant efforts, fragmented service delivery, and unnecessary administrative costs.

The result of such overlap is not just wasted money but also confusion for the individuals these programs are meant to serve. Job seekers, for instance, must navigate a complex web of programs to access training, often encountering inconsistent eligibility requirements and application processes. By consolidating these programs and creating a unified system, the government could reduce redundancy, streamline services, and save billions of dollars annually.

Outdated Processes and Technology

In many government agencies, outdated processes and technology are significant barriers to efficiency. Paper-based systems, legacy software, and manual workflows are still commonplace, despite the availability of modern tools that could drastically improve productivity and reduce costs.

The Internal Revenue Service (IRS) provides a striking example. The agency continues to rely on decades-old computer systems to process tax returns, leading to delays, errors, and increased costs. During the COVID-19 pandemic, the limitations of these systems became painfully evident when the IRS struggled to distribute stimulus payments quickly and accurately.

Modernizing technology across government agencies could not only improve service delivery but also reduce waste. For example, transitioning to digital records and automating routine tasks could save billions of dollars annually in administrative costs while enhancing transparency and accountability.

Procurement Inefficiencies

Government procurement is another area rife with inefficiencies. The process of acquiring goods and services is often slow, overly complex, and subject to excessive regulations. These challenges lead to inflated costs, delays in project completion, and sometimes the outright failure of critical initiatives.

One well-known example is the healthcare.gov website, which was plagued by technical issues and cost overruns during its rollout in 2013. The project's initial price tag of $93 million ballooned to over $1.7 billion, largely due to poor procurement practices and a lack of coordination among contractors. The fiasco highlighted the need for reforms to ensure that government contracts are awarded based on merit, accountability, and value rather than bureaucratic inertia.

The "Spend It or Lose It" Mentality

A pervasive cultural issue within government agencies is the "spend it or lose it" mentality, where departments rush to exhaust their budgets at the end of the fiscal year to avoid reductions in future allocations. This practice encourages wasteful expenditures on unnecessary items, from office supplies to travel expenses, simply to ensure that all allocated funds are spent.

For example, a study found that federal agencies spent nearly $50 billion in September 2018 alone—more than twice the monthly average—on items ranging from furniture to consulting services. While some of these expenditures may have been justified, the end-of-year spending surge raises questions about whether all purchases were truly necessary.

Addressing this issue requires a cultural shift within government agencies. Instead of penalizing departments for underspending, budgetary policies should reward efficiency and encourage savings. Creating mechanisms to carry over unspent funds to future fiscal years could help reduce the pressure to spend unnecessarily and promote more thoughtful financial planning.

Lack of Clear Performance Metrics

Another significant challenge is the lack of clear performance metrics for evaluating the effectiveness of government programs. Without measurable goals and regular assessments, it is difficult to determine whether a program is achieving its intended outcomes or if taxpayer dollars are being wasted.

For instance, a federal program designed to support small businesses was found to have issued grants without tracking how many jobs were created or businesses were launched as a result. This lack of accountability not only undermines the program's effectiveness but also makes it vulnerable to criticism and budget cuts.

Implementing performance-based budgeting, where funding levels are tied to measurable outcomes, could help address this issue. By requiring agencies to demonstrate the impact of their spending, policymakers can ensure that resources are allocated to programs that deliver results.

Conclusion and Transition

Bureaucratic inefficiencies are a major driver of wasteful government spending, costing taxpayers billions of dollars each year and undermining public trust in government institutions. From overlapping responsibilities and outdated technology to cultural issues and a lack of accountability, these inefficiencies represent both a challenge and an opportunity for meaningful reform.

In the next section, we will delve deeper into the cultural and structural changes needed to address these inefficiencies. By exploring innovative solutions and successful examples of reform, we can chart a path toward a more efficient, effective, and accountable government.

Addressing bureaucratic inefficiencies is no small task, as these issues are deeply embedded within the structure of government institutions. However, examples of successful reforms at various levels of government demonstrate that change is possible. By learning from these successes and adopting innovative approaches, we can reduce waste, streamline operations, and ensure that taxpayer dollars are used effectively.

Streamlining Agency Responsibilities

The overlap of responsibilities among federal agencies is a major source of inefficiency. Consolidating programs with similar objectives can lead to significant savings and improved service delivery. One notable success story is the streamlining of federal food safety oversight. Historically, food safety was managed by multiple agencies, including the Food and Drug Administration (FDA) and the Department of Agriculture (USDA), resulting in duplicative efforts and confusion.

In recent years, efforts to consolidate these responsibilities have led to better coordination and reduced redundancy. For example, the creation of the Food Safety Modernization Act empowered the FDA to take a more comprehensive approach to food safety, reducing the need for overlapping inspections and conflicting regulations. This reform not only improved efficiency but also enhanced public health outcomes by creating a clearer and more accountable system.

Modernizing Technology Across Agencies

Technology modernization is critical to eliminating inefficiencies and improving government operations. Some agencies have made significant strides in adopting modern tools and systems, serving as models for others.

For instance, the Department of Veterans Affairs (VA) launched an initiative to modernize its electronic health records (EHR) system, replacing outdated paper-based processes with a unified digital platform. This transition has improved the accuracy and accessibility of patient information, reducing errors and enabling faster deci-sion-making. While the project faced initial challenges, it ultimately demonstrated the potential of technology to transform how government agencies operate.

Other agencies, such as the General Services Administration (GSA), have embraced cloud computing and automation to streamline procurement processes and manage large-scale projects more efficiently. By investing in technology, these agencies have not only saved money but also improved the quality of services provided to the public.

Overhauling Procurement Practices

Procurement inefficiencies have long been a source of waste in government spending. However, innovative approaches have shown that reforms can deliver significant benefits. One example is the Defense Innovation Unit (DIU), an initiative launched by the Department of Defense to streamline the acquisition of cutting-edge technologies from the private sector.

The DIU bypasses traditional procurement processes, which are often slow and cumbersome, in favor of rapid contracting methods that enable the military to access new technologies more quickly. This approach has reduced costs, accelerated innovation, and improved the military's ability to respond to emerging threats.

At the local level, cities like Boston have adopted participatory procurement practices, allowing community stakeholders to weigh in on major purchasing decisions. This approach increases transparency, reduces the risk of corruption, and ensures that taxpayer dollars are spent on projects that align with public priorities.

Combating the "Spend It or Lose It" Mentality

Cultural change within government agencies is essential for addressing the "spend it or lose it" mentality that drives wasteful end-of-year expenditures. Some agencies have implemented policies to encourage fiscal responsibility and reward efficiency.

For example, the Department of Energy (DOE) introduced a pilot program that allows unspent funds to be rolled over into the next fiscal year. This change gives managers more flexibility in budgeting and reduces the pressure to exhaust budgets unnecessarily. Early results from the program indicate that it has led to more thoughtful spending decisions and significant cost savings.

Implementing Performance-Based Budgeting
Performance-based budgeting ties funding levels to measurable outcomes, creating incentives for agencies to focus on efficiency and results. This approach has been successfully implemented in several states and local governments.

One notable example is the state of Washington, which adopted a performance-based budgeting system to address its fiscal challenges. Agencies are required to develop clear performance metrics and demonstrate how their spending contributes to achieving specific goals. This approach has improved accountability and allowed lawmakers to make more informed decisions about resource allocation.

Fostering Public Engagement and Transparency

Engaging the public in government decision-making is another effective way to combat inefficiencies and ensure accountability. Participatory budgeting programs, where residents have a direct say in how a portion of public funds is spent, have been successful in cities around the world.

For example, New York City's participatory budgeting initiative allows citizens to propose and vote on community projects, such as park improvements or school upgrades. By involving residents in the process, the city has increased transparency and ensured that funds are allocated to projects that reflect community priorities.

At the federal level, transparency initiatives such as USAspending. gov provide taxpayers with detailed information about government expenditures. Expanding and enhancing these tools can empower citizens to hold officials accountable and advocate for more efficient use of public funds.

The Potential of Artificial Intelligence and Automation

Emerging technologies like artificial intelligence (AI) and automation offer new opportunities to address bureaucratic inefficiencies.

AI-powered tools can analyze vast amounts of data to identify patterns, detect fraud, and optimize resource allocation. For example, the Social Security Administration has used AI to streamline claims processing, reducing wait times and saving millions of dollars annually.

Automation can also eliminate repetitive tasks, freeing up staff to focus on more complex and strategic activities. By embracing these technologies, government agencies can reduce costs, improve accuracy, and enhance the quality of public services.

Conclusion and Transition

The examples of successful reforms and innovative approaches discussed in this section demonstrate that addressing bureaucratic inefficiencies is both necessary and achievable. Streamlining agency responsibilities, modernizing technology, overhauling procurement practices, and fostering a culture of accountability can lead to significant improvements in the efficiency and effectiveness of government operations.

In the next section, we will explore the broader cultural and structural changes needed to create a government that prioritizes fiscal responsibility and public trust. By building on the lessons learned from successful reforms, we can chart a path toward a more accountable and effective system of governance.

Addressing the root causes of wasteful spending requires not just reforming systems but also reshaping the culture within government agencies. The persistence of inefficiencies is often a result of long-standing habits, resistance to change, and a lack of incentives to innovate. By fostering a culture of fiscal responsibility, transparency, and accountability, governments can create an environment where efficiency and effectiveness are prioritized.

The Need for Leadership in Driving Change
Leadership plays a critical role in setting the tone for how government agencies operate. Strong leaders can challenge the status quo, push for reforms, and inspire employees to embrace a culture of efficiency. Conversely, a lack of leadership can perpetuate inefficiencies and allow wasteful practices to persist.

One notable example of leadership-driven reform is the city of Baltimore's adoption of CitiStat, a performance management program designed to improve accountability and efficiency across city departments. Under this system, agency leaders were required to regularly report on key performance metrics, such as crime rates, waste collection efficiency, and infrastructure repairs. This data-driven approach enabled the city to identify inefficiencies, allocate resources more effectively, and save millions of dollars.

The success of CitiStat highlights the importance of leadership in driving change. By setting clear expectations, providing resources for innovation, and holding employees accountable, leaders can foster a culture of continuous improvement within government agencies.

Encouraging Innovation Through Incentives
Innovation is often stifled in government agencies due to a lack of incentives and the perception that taking risks could lead to failure. To address this, governments should create systems that reward employees for proposing and implementing cost-saving measures.

For example, some states have introduced employee suggestion programs that offer monetary rewards or public recognition for ideas that reduce costs or improve efficiency. One program in Tennessee saved millions of dollars by implementing employee-proposed changes to procurement and energy usage practices. These initiatives not only promote innovation but also empower employees to take ownership of their roles in improving government operations.

In addition to employee incentives, governments can establish innovation labs or task forces dedicated to identifying and testing new approaches to service delivery. These teams can pilot initiatives on a small scale, evaluate their effectiveness, and expand successful programs across agencies.

Breaking Down Silos Between Agencies
Silos within government agencies are a significant barrier to efficiency. Departments often operate independently, with little collab-

oration or communication, leading to redundant efforts and wasted resources. Breaking down these silos requires fostering a culture of cooperation and shared responsibility.

One approach is the establishment of interagency task forces to address cross-cutting issues such as climate change, public health, or infrastructure development. These task forces bring together representatives from multiple agencies to share expertise, align goals, and coordinate efforts. For example, the Federal Emergency Management Agency (FEMA) has worked with state and local governments to create unified disaster response plans, improving resource allocation and reducing duplication of efforts.

Technology can also play a role in breaking down silos. Integrated data systems allow agencies to share information and collaborate more effectively. For instance, a shared database for housing assistance programs can help multiple agencies identify overlapping services, reduce administrative costs, and provide better support to citizens in need.

The Role of Transparency in Building Public Trust
Transparency is a cornerstone of accountability and a powerful tool for fostering public trust. When citizens have access to information about how their tax dollars are being spent, they are better equipped to hold officials accountable and advocate for change.

One successful example of transparency in action is the state of Ohio's launch of OhioCheckbook.com, an online platform that provides detailed information about state and local government expenditures. The platform allows taxpayers to see exactly how their money is being used, from salaries to capital projects. This level of transparency has not only increased public confidence but also encouraged government officials to be more mindful of their spending.

Expanding such platforms at the federal level could have a transformative impact on accountability. By making data accessible and user-friendly, governments can empower citizens to play an active role in monitoring expenditures and advocating for reforms.

The Importance of Citizen Engagement

Engaging citizens in decision-making processes is another critical strategy for addressing bureaucratic inefficiencies. Participatory budgeting programs, which allow residents to propose and vote on funding priorities, have proven effective in ensuring that government resources are aligned with community needs.

For instance, Chicago has implemented participatory budgeting in several wards, giving residents the opportunity to allocate a portion of their aldermanic discretionary funds. Projects funded through this process have included new streetlights, public art installations, and improvements to community centers. By involving citizens directly, participatory budgeting increases transparency, reduces waste, and fosters a sense of shared responsibility for public resources.

Beyond budgeting, citizen engagement can extend to program evaluation and policy development. Governments can use surveys, focus groups, and public forums to gather input on existing programs and identify areas for improvement. This collaborative approach not only enhances efficiency but also strengthens the relationship between citizens and their government.

Overcoming Resistance to Change

Implementing reforms often faces resistance from within government agencies, where employees may fear job losses, increased workloads, or changes to established routines. Addressing this resistance requires a thoughtful approach that includes clear communication, training, and support.

Leaders must articulate the benefits of reforms and involve employees in the process, ensuring that their concerns are heard and addressed. Providing training on new systems or processes can ease transitions and equip employees with the skills they need to succeed. Additionally, recognizing and rewarding employees who embrace change can help build momentum for broader cultural shifts.

Conclusion and Transition

Reshaping the culture within government agencies is a critical step toward reducing wasteful spending and improving efficiency. By fostering leadership, encouraging innovation, promoting transparency, and engaging citizens, governments can create an environment where accountability and fiscal responsibility thrive.

In the next section, we will explore how these cultural and structural reforms can be scaled and sustained over time, ensuring that progress is not only achieved but also maintained. By examining case studies and best practices, we can chart a path toward a more effective and accountable government system.

Building a government that is efficient, accountable, and responsive to citizens' needs requires scaling reforms and sustaining progress over time. Achieving these goals involves institutionalizing best practices, leveraging innovative solutions, and creating systems that are resilient to backsliding. Governments at all levels have successfully implemented reforms, offering valuable lessons for ensuring that efficiency becomes a lasting priority.

Institutionalizing Best Practices

One of the most effective ways to sustain reform is to institutionalize best practices through formal policies and procedures. This approach ensures that improvements are not dependent on individual leaders or political cycles but become embedded in the fabric of government operations.

For example, the state of Oregon implemented a performance-based budgeting system that requires all agencies to align their funding requests with measurable outcomes. By mandating this process through legislation, the state has ensured that efficiency and accountability remain central to its budgeting practices, regardless of changes in leadership.

Similarly, some cities have codified participatory budgeting programs into their municipal charters, making citizen engagement a permanent feature of the budgeting process. These institutionalized reforms create a framework for sustained accountability and provide a foundation for continuous improvement.

Leveraging Data and Analytics

Data and analytics play a critical role in sustaining progress by enabling governments to identify inefficiencies, measure performance, and make evidence-based decisions. Advances in technology have made it possible to collect and analyze data at an unprecedented scale, offering new opportunities to improve efficiency and transparency.

For instance, New York City's Mayor's Office of Data Analytics (MODA) uses data to identify trends and allocate resources more effectively. By analyzing data on emergency response times, housing inspections, and public health outcomes, MODA has helped the city save millions of dollars while improving services for residents.

To scale these successes, governments can invest in building data capabilities across agencies. This includes training employees in data analysis, adopting standardized data-sharing protocols, and creating centralized platforms for monitoring performance. By embedding data-driven decision-making into everyday operations, governments can ensure that efficiency becomes a core principle of governance.

Scaling Innovation Across Agencies
Innovation often begins with pilot programs or isolated initiatives, but scaling these efforts across multiple agencies is key to maximizing their impact. Successful scaling requires clear communication, robust evaluation, and a commitment to adapting solutions to different contexts.

One example of successful scaling is the federal government's adoption of shared services for administrative functions, such as human resources and financial management. By consolidating these services across agencies, the government has reduced duplication, improved efficiency, and saved billions of dollars. Expanding shared services to additional functions, such as procurement or IT support, could yield even greater savings.

Another promising approach is the use of innovation labs to test and refine new ideas before scaling them. For example, the U.S. Digital Service (USDS) works with federal agencies to develop and implement technology solutions that improve service delivery. By starting small and building on success, the USDS has demonstrated how innovation can be scaled effectively across government.

Creating Feedback Loops for Continuous Improvement
Sustaining progress also requires creating feedback loops that allow governments to evaluate the impact of reforms and make adjustments as needed. Regular audits, performance reviews, and citizen feedback mechanisms are essential for identifying areas where improvements are needed and ensuring that reforms remain relevant over time.

For instance, the state of Colorado conducts annual performance reviews of its agencies, focusing on metrics such as cost savings, service delivery, and customer satisfaction. These reviews provide valuable insights into what is working and what isn't, enabling the state to refine its strategies and maintain momentum for reform.

Feedback loops also play a critical role in fostering public trust. When citizens see that their input is valued and leads to tangible improvements, they are more likely to support government initiatives and engage in civic life.

Building Resilience to Backsliding
One of the biggest challenges in sustaining reform is preventing backsliding, particularly during leadership transitions or periods of economic uncertainty. Building resilience to backsliding requires creating systems that are self-reinforcing and resistant to external pressures.

For example, independent oversight bodies, such as inspectors general or audit offices, can act as safeguards against inefficiency and corruption. By operating independently of political influence, these bodies provide an impartial check on government operations and ensure that reforms are upheld.

Another strategy is to establish bipartisan or nonpartisan commissions to oversee key areas of government spending, such as infrastructure or healthcare. These commissions can provide continuity and stability, ensuring that reforms are not undone by political shifts.

Engaging the Private Sector and Nonprofits

Partnerships with the private sector and nonprofit organizations can also play a role in sustaining progress. These partnerships bring additional expertise, resources, and perspectives to the table, enabling governments to tackle complex challenges more effectively.

For example, public-private partnerships (PPPs) have been used to deliver major infrastructure projects, such as highways and public transit systems, at lower costs and with greater efficiency. Nonprofit organizations, meanwhile, have collaborated with governments on initiatives ranging from homelessness prevention to environmental conservation, leveraging their specialized knowledge and networks to drive impact.

By fostering collaboration with external partners, governments can enhance their capacity for innovation and ensure that reforms are sustainable over the long term.

Conclusion and Transition

Sustaining progress in addressing bureaucratic inefficiencies requires a multifaceted approach that combines institutional reform, data-driven decision-making, and collaboration across sectors. By learning from successful examples and scaling best practices, governments can create systems that are not only efficient but also resilient to future challenges.

In the next chapter, we will explore the role of citizen advocacy in driving reform. From grassroots movements to policy advocacy, citizens have a critical role to play in holding governments accountable and ensuring that taxpayer dollars are used responsibly.

Chapter 5: The Role of Citizen Advocacy

Government wasteful spending does not occur in a vacuum—it thrives in an environment of low accountability and limited public scrutiny. While reforms and structural changes are essential, they are unlikely to succeed without active engagement from citizens. Advocacy by taxpayers, grassroots organizations, and watchdog groups plays a pivotal role in holding governments accountable and ensuring that public funds are used responsibly. This chapter explores how citizen advocacy can drive meaningful change and empower communities to demand better governance.

Why Citizen Advocacy Matters

Citizen advocacy is the foundation of a functioning democracy. Governments are accountable to the people, but this accountability depends on an engaged and informed public. Advocacy efforts ensure that citizens have a voice in decision-making processes and that their concerns are heard by policymakers.

Without advocacy, inefficiencies and waste can go unchecked, allowing government spending to drift away from the priorities of the public. Citizen advocacy creates pressure for transparency and accountability, compelling officials to justify their decisions and demonstrate how taxpayer dollars are being spent.

Grassroots Movements for Change

Grassroots movements have historically been among the most effective drivers of government reform. These movements often begin with local concerns but can grow to address broader issues of waste, corruption, or inefficiency. Their strength lies in their ability to mobilize ordinary citizens and amplify their voices through collective action.

One notable example is the push for participatory budgeting in U.S. cities. What started as a local initiative in Chicago has spread to municipalities across the country, empowering residents to have a direct say in how public funds are allocated. By giving citizens a tangible role in budget decisions, participatory budgeting fosters transparency and ensures that spending aligns with community priorities.

Another powerful grassroots effort is the "Open Data" movement, which advocates for public access to government spending information. This movement has led to the creation of online platforms like USAspending.gov, where taxpayers can track federal expenditures in detail. These tools have not only increased transparency but also provided citizens with the information needed to advocate for smarter spending decisions.

The Role of Watchdog Organizations

Watchdog organizations play a crucial role in identifying wasteful spending and bringing it to public attention. Groups such as the Government Accountability Office (GAO), Citizens Against Government Waste (CAGW), and local audit offices serve as independent monitors of government activity. Their reports often uncover inefficiencies, highlight questionable expenditures, and recommend reforms.

For example, CAGW's annual "Pig Book" highlights the most egregious examples of pork-barrel spending in the federal budget. By publishing this information in an accessible format, CAGW equips citizens with the knowledge to challenge wasteful practices and demand greater accountability from their representatives.

At the local level, state auditors often conduct detailed reviews of agency operations, identifying areas where improvements can be made. These reports are valuable tools for citizens and advocacy groups, providing concrete evidence to support calls for reform.

Engaging with Elected Officials

Citizens have the power to influence government spending by engaging directly with elected officials. Writing letters, attending town hall meetings, and participating in public comment periods are all effective ways to make concerns known and hold representatives accountable.

For example, when a controversial infrastructure project was proposed in a mid-sized U.S. city, local residents organized a campaign to voice their opposition. They attended city council meetings, presented data on the project's costs and benefits, and ultimately convinced officials to redirect funds to more pressing community needs. This case demonstrates the impact that organized, informed advocacy can have on government decision-making.

Engaging with officials also includes voting for candidates who prioritize fiscal responsibility and transparency. Citizens can influence the direction of government spending by supporting leaders who are committed to reducing waste and improving efficiency.

The Power of Social Media

Social media has become an indispensable tool for citizen advocacy, allowing individuals and organizations to reach wide audiences and mobilize quickly. Platforms like Twitter, Facebook, and Instagram provide a space for sharing information, organizing events, and raising awareness about wasteful spending.

For example, when news broke about a $43 million gas station built in Afghanistan, social media outrage helped amplify the story, prompting investigations and public accountability. Similarly, grassroots campaigns often use hashtags to rally support for causes, such as #NoMoreWaste or #AccountabilityNow, creating momentum for change.

Social media also enables real-time engagement with policymakers. Many elected officials use platforms like Twitter to communicate with constituents, providing an opportunity for citizens to ask questions, share concerns, and advocate for better spending practices.

Educating and Mobilizing Communities

Education is a cornerstone of effective advocacy. Citizens are more likely to engage when they understand how government spending affects their lives and what they can do to influence it. Advocacy organizations and community leaders can play a vital role in educating the public about budgeting processes, the impact of wasteful spending, and opportunities for engagement.

Workshops, seminars, and informational campaigns are effective ways to build awareness and mobilize communities. For example, a nonprofit organization focused on public accountability might host a webinar explaining how to analyze a city's budget or write a public records request. By equipping citizens with knowledge and tools, these efforts empower individuals to take action.

Overcoming Challenges to Advocacy
While citizen advocacy is powerful, it is not without challenges. Apathy, misinformation, and barriers to participation can limit the effectiveness of advocacy efforts. Governments can address these challenges by fostering a culture of inclusion and actively encouraging public engagement.

For example, simplifying the language used in budget documents and providing accessible summaries can make it easier for citizens to understand complex financial information. Offering multiple avenues for participation—such as online comment forms, virtual town halls, and in-person meetings—can ensure that diverse voices are heard.

Conclusion and Transition
Citizen advocacy is a cornerstone of accountability in government spending. By engaging with elected officials, mobilizing through grassroots movements, and leveraging tools like social media and watchdog reports, citizens can drive meaningful change and reduce waste. Advocacy efforts not only ensure that taxpayer dollars are used responsibly but also strengthen the relationship between governments and the people they serve.

In the next section, we will examine specific examples of successful citizen advocacy campaigns and the lessons they offer for future efforts. From local initiatives to national movements, these stories demonstrate the transformative power of collective action.

Citizen advocacy has a proven track record of driving meaningful reforms in government spending. Across the United States and around the world, communities have mobilized to hold officials accountable, expose waste, and demand better use of taxpayer dollars. These stories of successful advocacy not only inspire but also provide valuable lessons for future efforts.

Participatory Budgeting in New York City
New York City is a shining example of how participatory budgeting can empower citizens to influence government spending. Introduced in 2011, the initiative allocates a portion of council members' discretionary budgets to projects proposed and voted on by residents. These funds have been used for a wide range of community improvements, from installing safer pedestrian crossings to upgrading school facilities.

The process begins with residents submitting project ideas, which are then reviewed for feasibility by city staff. Once the proposals are finalized, community members vote to decide which projects will receive funding. The program has been praised for its transparency and inclusivity, as it engages residents who might otherwise feel disconnected from government decision-making.

Participatory budgeting demonstrates the power of involving citizens in financial decisions. By giving taxpayers a direct say in how public funds are spent, the initiative fosters trust and ensures that spending aligns with community priorities. Its success has inspired other cities across the U.S. to adopt similar programs, proving that grassroots advocacy can lead to systemic change.

Stopping the Bridge to Nowhere

One of the most well-known examples of citizen advocacy against wasteful spending is the opposition to Alaska's infamous "bridge to nowhere." The proposed $398 million project aimed to connect the small town of Ketchikan to Gravina Island, home to just 50 residents. Critics argued that the cost was disproportionate to the potential benefits and represented a blatant example of pork-barrel spending.

The project faced widespread backlash from taxpayers, watchdog organizations, and media outlets. Advocacy groups like Citizens Against Government Waste (CAGW) highlighted the project in their reports, bringing national attention to the issue. Public pressure eventually led Congress to reallocate the funds to other infrastructure needs.

This case underscores the importance of vigilance and collective action in combating wasteful spending. By shining a spotlight on questionable expenditures, citizens can compel lawmakers to re-evaluate their priorities and make more responsible decisions.

Exposing Fraud in Pandemic Relief Programs
The COVID-19 pandemic saw unprecedented levels of government spending to address public health and economic crises. While these efforts were necessary, they were also prone to waste and fraud due to the urgency of disbursing funds quickly. Advocacy groups and investigative journalists played a crucial role in identifying instances of misuse and pushing for greater accountability.

One example is the Paycheck Protection Program (PPP), which provided loans to businesses to help retain employees during the pandemic. Reports revealed that billions of dollars were issued to ineligible recipients, including fake businesses and large corporations that exploited loopholes. Advocacy groups called for stricter oversight, and public pressure led to the recovery of some funds and the implementation of additional safeguards.

This case highlights the value of citizen engagement during times of crisis. By demanding accountability, taxpayers can help ensure that emergency funds are directed to those who need them most and are not lost to fraud or mismanagement.

Advocating for Public Infrastructure in Flint, Michigan
The water crisis in Flint, Michigan, is a tragic example of how waste and mismanagement can harm communities. However, it also illustrates the power of citizen advocacy in holding officials accountable and driving change.

When residents discovered that their water supply was contaminated with lead, they organized protests, filed lawsuits, and reached out to media outlets to bring attention to the crisis. Advocacy efforts eventually led to federal and state investigations, significant financial settlements for affected families, and the allocation of funds to replace Flint's aging water infrastructure.

The Flint water crisis serves as a reminder that citizen advocacy is not only about preventing waste but also about demanding justice and equitable access to essential services. It also demonstrates the importance of perseverance, as it took years of sustained effort to achieve meaningful progress.

Lessons from Advocacy Success Stories
These examples of successful advocacy share several common elements that can serve as a blueprint for future efforts:

Awareness and Education: Effective advocacy begins with raising awareness about the issue. Providing clear, accessible information about wasteful spending helps build public support and mobilize action.
Collective Action: Advocacy is most effective when individuals and organizations work together. Grassroots movements, coalitions, and partnerships amplify voices and increase pressure on deci-sion-makers.
Persistence: Change rarely happens overnight. Sustained advoca-cy, even in the face of resistance, is essential for achieving long-term success.
Leverage Technology: Social media, online petitions, and da-ta-sharing platforms can help advocates reach wider audiences and organize more effectively.
Engage with Policymakers: Direct engagement with elected offi-cials, through letters, meetings, and public testimony, ensures that advocacy efforts are heard by those in positions of power.
Conclusion and Transition
Citizen advocacy has the power to expose waste, hold officials accountable, and drive meaningful reform. The success stories discussed in this chapter demonstrate that when taxpayers come together to demand change, they can influence government spend-ing and improve public services.

In the next section, we will explore strategies for scaling these ef-forts, focusing on how individuals and organizations can collaborate to create a national movement for accountability and fiscal respon-sibility.

Scaling citizen advocacy from local efforts to a national movement requires organization, coordination, and a commitment to sustained

action. While individual advocacy campaigns can achieve significant victories, a broader, unified approach has the potential to
create systemic change. This page explores how grassroots organizations, technology, and partnerships can come together to build
a national movement for accountability and fiscal responsibility in
government spending.

Building Coalitions for Greater Impact
One of the most effective ways to scale advocacy efforts is by building coalitions that unite individuals and organizations with shared
goals. Coalitions amplify voices, pool resources, and provide a platform for coordinated action, increasing their collective impact.

For example, the coalition formed to advocate for transparency in
federal spending brought together watchdog organizations, policy
think tanks, and community groups. This collaboration was instrumental in the creation of the Federal Funding Accountability and
Transparency Act (FFATA) of 2006, which established the ground-
work for platforms like USAspending.gov. By leveraging the expertise and networks of its members, the coalition was able to influence policymakers and drive legislative change.

Coalitions also provide a framework for sharing best practices and
learning from successful advocacy campaigns. Regular communication, joint campaigns, and coordinated messaging ensure that
efforts are aligned and mutually reinforcing, maximizing their effectiveness.

Leveraging Technology for Advocacy
Technology is a powerful tool for organizing, educating, and mobilizing citizens. Advocacy groups can use digital platforms to reach
wider audiences, streamline communication, and facilitate action.

Social Media Campaigns: Platforms like Twitter, Facebook, and Instagram enable advocates to raise awareness, share updates, and
engage directly with supporters. Hashtags like #StopTheWaste or
#FiscalResponsibility can help campaigns gain traction and reach
new audiences.
Petition Platforms: Online petition sites like Change.org allow advocates to gather support quickly and demonstrate public backing for

their cause. High-profile petitions can attract media attention and put pressure on policymakers.

Crowdsourcing Solutions: Platforms like IdeaScale enable citizens to propose and vote on solutions to public issues. Governments can use these platforms to engage directly with constituents, fostering collaboration and transparency.

Technology also enables real-time data sharing, which can be critical for identifying and addressing wasteful spending. For instance, mobile apps that allow citizens to report instances of inefficiency or fraud can provide valuable insights to advocacy groups and watchdog organizations.

Engaging Younger Generations

To build a sustainable movement, it is essential to engage younger generations in advocacy efforts. Millennials and Generation Z are often passionate about social justice, transparency, and accountability, making them natural allies in the fight against wasteful spending.

Educational initiatives, such as workshops and classroom programs, can help younger citizens understand how government spending affects their lives and how they can influence it. Partnerships with schools, universities, and youth organizations can provide opportunities for civic engagement and leadership development.

Social media and digital platforms are particularly effective for reaching younger audiences. Advocacy campaigns that incorporate interactive content, such as videos, quizzes, and infographics, can educate and inspire action among tech-savvy generations.

The Role of Data Journalism

Data journalism is another powerful tool for scaling advocacy efforts. By analyzing and visualizing government spending data, journalists can uncover patterns, highlight inefficiencies, and bring wasteful practices to public attention.

One notable example is ProPublica's investigative reporting on federal spending, which has exposed fraud, mismanagement, and questionable expenditures across various agencies. These reports

not only inform the public but also provide advocates with evidence
to support their campaigns.

Collaborations between advocacy groups and data journalists can
enhance the impact of both. While journalists provide the research
and storytelling, advocates can use the findings to mobilize citizens
and pressure policymakers.

Creating a National Advocacy Network

Establishing a national network of advocacy groups can provide
a unified platform for addressing wasteful spending. This network
could coordinate efforts across local, state, and federal levels, ensuring that campaigns are aligned and mutually reinforcing.

Key components of a national advocacy network might include:

Centralized Resources: A shared database of best practices, research, and campaign materials that all members can access.
Regular Communication: Weekly or monthly calls to share updates,
discuss challenges, and plan joint campaigns.
National Days of Action: Coordinated events, such as marches,
town halls, or social media blitzes, to raise awareness and demonstrate public support.
Such a network would not only amplify the impact of individual efforts but also create a sense of solidarity among advocates,
strengthening the movement as a whole.

Measuring Success and Building Momentum

To sustain a national movement, it is important to measure success
and celebrate victories. Tracking metrics such as policy changes,
reductions in wasteful spending, and increased public engagement
can demonstrate the effectiveness of advocacy efforts and motivate
participants to stay involved.

Highlighting success stories—such as the reallocation of funds from
the "bridge to nowhere" or the creation of participatory budgeting
programs—can inspire others to join the movement and replicate
successful strategies in their own communities.

Conclusion and Transition

Scaling citizen advocacy to a national level requires organization, innovation, and collaboration. By leveraging technology, engaging younger generations, and building coalitions, advocates can create a powerful movement for accountability and fiscal responsibility.

In the next section, we will explore the challenges and obstacles that advocacy campaigns often face, as well as strategies for overcoming them. From political resistance to public apathy, understanding these barriers is essential for ensuring the success of citizen-led reform efforts.

While citizen advocacy has the power to drive meaningful reforms, it is not without challenges. Advocacy campaigns often face obstacles ranging from political resistance to public apathy. Overcoming these barriers requires strategic thinking, persistence, and a willingness to adapt. This page explores common challenges faced by advocacy efforts and offers strategies for addressing them effectively.

Challenge 1: Political Resistance
One of the most significant barriers to advocacy is resistance from political leaders and institutions. Elected officials may be reluctant to acknowledge wasteful spending, particularly if it involves projects that benefit their constituencies or align with their political agendas. Additionally, entrenched bureaucracies often resist change due to fear of disruption or job losses.

Strategies for Overcoming Political Resistance:

Build Public Pressure: When elected officials face overwhelming public demand for reform, they are more likely to act. Advocacy campaigns should focus on mobilizing citizens to contact their representatives, attend town hall meetings, and participate in public demonstrations.
Engage Allies in Government: Not all officials resist change. Identifying and working with reform-minded policymakers can help advance advocacy goals. These allies can champion reforms within government and lend credibility to advocacy efforts.
Use Data and Evidence: Providing clear, well-researched evidence of wasteful spending can make it harder for officials to dismiss advocacy efforts. Reports, case studies, and cost-benefit analyses are

valuable tools for building a compelling case for reform.
Challenge 2: Public Apathy
Engaging the public in advocacy efforts can be difficult, particularly when issues like wasteful spending seem abstract or disconnected from everyday life. Many citizens feel powerless to influence government decisions, leading to disengagement and apathy.

Strategies for Overcoming Public Apathy:

Make It Personal: Advocacy campaigns should highlight how wasteful spending directly impacts citizens' lives, such as by reducing funding for schools, healthcare, or infrastructure. Personal stories and relatable examples can make the issue more tangible and compelling.
Use Accessible Language: Government budgets and spending reports are often filled with jargon and technical terms. Simplifying this information and presenting it in user-friendly formats—such as infographics or videos—can make it more engaging for the public.
Leverage Social Media: Social media platforms are powerful tools for reaching and engaging diverse audiences. Campaigns that use creative content, such as memes, hashtags, and interactive polls, can generate interest and spark conversations.
Challenge 3: Fragmented Advocacy Efforts
Advocacy campaigns are often fragmented, with multiple groups working independently on similar issues. This lack of coordination can dilute efforts, create competition for resources, and confuse the public.

Strategies for Fostering Collaboration:

Create Coalitions: Forming coalitions that unite organizations with shared goals can increase the impact of advocacy efforts. Coalitions provide a platform for resource sharing, coordinated messaging, and joint campaigns.
Host Conferences and Workshops: Regular events that bring together advocates, policymakers, and community leaders can foster collaboration and build momentum for reform.
Develop Shared Goals: Establishing a common agenda with specific, measurable objectives can align efforts and ensure that all parties are working toward the same outcomes.

Challenge 4: Misinformation and Polarization
Misinformation and political polarization can undermine advocacy efforts by distorting the facts and dividing public opinion. In some cases, opponents of reform may spread false information to discredit advocacy campaigns or create confusion about the issues at hand.

Strategies for Combating Misinformation:

Fact-Check and Correct Errors: Advocacy groups should monitor public discourse and correct inaccuracies with verified information. Publishing fact sheets, FAQs, and rebuttals can help counter misinformation.
Focus on Nonpartisan Messaging: Framing advocacy efforts as nonpartisan and focused on common goals—such as fiscal responsibility and government accountability—can help bridge divides and build broad support.
Engage Trusted Voices: Partnering with respected community leaders, academics, and journalists can lend credibility to advocacy efforts and ensure that accurate information reaches the public.
Challenge 5: Resource Constraints
Advocacy efforts often operate with limited resources, which can make it difficult to sustain campaigns, conduct research, or engage with policymakers effectively.

Strategies for Addressing Resource Constraints:

Seek Grants and Donations: Many foundations and philanthropic organizations offer funding for advocacy efforts focused on government accountability and transparency. Applying for grants or launching crowdfunding campaigns can provide much-needed support.
Leverage Volunteer Networks: Recruiting volunteers to assist with outreach, event planning, and research can help stretch limited budgets.
Use Low-Cost Tools: Digital platforms like Canva, Zoom, and Mailchimp offer affordable solutions for creating materials, hosting events, and managing communication.
Challenge 6: Sustaining Momentum
Sustaining advocacy efforts over time can be challenging, partic-

ularly when progress is slow or resistance is strong. Maintaining enthusiasm and engagement requires a long-term strategy.

Strategies for Sustaining Momentum:

Celebrate Milestones: Recognizing and celebrating small victories, such as securing a meeting with policymakers or reaching a fund-raising goal, can keep advocates motivated.
Provide Regular Updates: Keeping supporters informed about progress, challenges, and next steps helps maintain engagement and builds trust.
Foster a Sense of Community: Creating opportunities for advocates to connect, share experiences, and support one another can strengthen the movement and ensure its longevity.
Conclusion and Transition
Overcoming the challenges of advocacy requires persistence, creativity, and collaboration. By addressing political resistance, public apathy, and other obstacles head-on, citizens can build powerful movements that hold governments accountable and reduce wasteful spending.

In the next section, we will explore the tools and technologies that can empower advocates and enhance the effectiveness of their campaigns. From data analytics to social media, these tools offer new opportunities for driving change in an increasingly digital world.

Citizen advocacy campaigns are increasingly leveraging tools and technologies to enhance their impact and reach. From data analytics to social media platforms, these tools enable advocates to mobilize supporters, uncover inefficiencies, and influence policymakers more effectively. This page explores how these technologies are transforming advocacy and empowering citizens to demand better governance.

Data Analytics: Turning Information into Action
Data analytics has become a cornerstone of modern advocacy, providing advocates with the tools to analyze government spending, identify inefficiencies, and develop evidence-based solutions. By turning raw data into actionable insights, advocates can build compelling cases for reform and engage the public in meaningful ways.

Spending Analysis: Platforms like USAspending.gov and OpenThe-Books.com allow citizens to explore detailed information about government expenditures. Advocates can use these tools to uncover questionable spending, such as redundant programs or overpriced contracts, and present their findings to the public and policymakers.

Trend Identification: Data analytics can reveal patterns in government spending, such as end-of-year surges or recurring inefficiencies in specific agencies. These insights enable advocates to target their efforts where they will have the greatest impact.

Visualization Tools: Visualizing data through charts, graphs, and maps makes complex information easier to understand and share. Tools like Tableau and Microsoft Power BI can help advocates create compelling presentations that resonate with diverse audiences.

Social Media: Amplifying Advocacy Efforts

Social media platforms are powerful tools for spreading awareness, mobilizing supporters, and engaging with policymakers. By leveraging the reach and immediacy of platforms like Twitter, Facebook, and Instagram, advocates can build momentum for their campaigns and connect with a broader audience.

Hashtag Campaigns: Creating and promoting hashtags, such as #StopTheWaste or #TransparentTaxation, helps advocates unify their messaging and make their campaigns more discoverable.

Live Streaming: Platforms like Facebook Live and Instagram Live enable advocates to host virtual events, such as town halls or panel discussions, that engage supporters in real time.

Policymaker Engagement: Many elected officials use social media to communicate with constituents. Advocates can use these platforms to share their concerns, ask questions, and encourage others to join the conversation.

Crowdsourcing and Collaboration Tools

Crowdsourcing platforms provide opportunities for citizens to contribute ideas, report issues, and collaborate on solutions. These tools democratize the advocacy process, allowing individuals to play an active role in shaping campaigns and driving change.

Crowdsourced Reporting: Mobile apps like SeeClickFix allow citizens to report local government inefficiencies, such as potholes or broken streetlights. These reports can be aggregated to identify broader trends and inform advocacy efforts.

Idea Sharing Platforms: Tools like IdeaScale enable communities to propose and vote on solutions to public challenges. This collaborative approach fosters innovation and ensures that advocacy efforts reflect the needs and priorities of the public.

Petition Sites: Platforms like Change.org and Care2 make it easy to launch and promote petitions, gather signatures, and demonstrate public support for specific reforms.

Digital Advocacy Campaigns

Digital advocacy campaigns combine multiple tools and strategies to create cohesive, impactful initiatives. These campaigns often include websites, email newsletters, and social media content that inform and engage the public while driving specific calls to action.

Interactive Websites: Advocacy websites can serve as hubs for information, providing visitors with resources such as policy briefs, toolkits, and contact information for elected officials.

Email Outreach: Email campaigns allow advocates to communicate directly with supporters, sharing updates, calls to action, and success stories.

Targeted Advertising: Digital advertising platforms, such as Google Ads or Facebook Ads, enable advocates to reach specific audiences based on demographics, interests, and location.

Artificial Intelligence and Automation

Emerging technologies like artificial intelligence (AI) and automation are opening new possibilities for advocacy. These tools can streamline processes, enhance communication, and uncover insights that were previously inaccessible.

Chatbots: AI-powered chatbots can answer frequently asked questions, guide users through complex issues, and encourage them to take action, such as signing a petition or contacting their representatives.

Sentiment Analysis: AI tools can analyze public sentiment on social media and other platforms, helping advocates gauge the effectiveness of their campaigns and adjust their strategies accordingly.

Automated Reporting: Automation can streamline the creation of reports and newsletters, freeing up advocates to focus on strategy and engagement.

Building a Future of Accountable Governance

The integration of technology into citizen advocacy efforts is transforming the way campaigns are organized and executed. By harnessing the power of data, social media, and emerging tools, advocates can amplify their voices, connect with broader audiences, and drive meaningful change.

However, the effectiveness of these tools ultimately depends on the people who use them. Advocacy campaigns must remain focused on their goals, grounded in evidence, and committed to transparency and accountability. By combining technology with passion and persistence, citizens can build a future where government spending reflects the values and priorities of the people it serves.

Conclusion and Transition

Citizen advocacy, empowered by technology, has the potential to transform governance and reduce wasteful spending. In the next chapter, we will examine how governments can partner with citizens and organizations to create a culture of accountability. By fostering collaboration and building trust, governments and citizens can work together to achieve a more efficient and equitable system of public spending.

Chapter 6: Collaborating for Accountability

Reducing wasteful government spending and fostering accountability is not a task for governments alone. Effective governance requires collaboration between public institutions, private organizations, and citizens. By building partnerships and leveraging shared resources, these groups can work together to create a culture of fiscal responsibility, transparency, and trust. This chapter explores how collaborative efforts can strengthen accountability and ensure that taxpayer dollars are used effectively.

The Importance of Collaboration

Collaboration between governments and external stakeholders brings diverse perspectives, expertise, and resources to the table. It also creates checks and balances that help prevent waste and inefficiency. By involving citizens, businesses, and nonprofit organizations in decision-making processes, governments can ensure that spending decisions align with public needs and priorities.

Collaboration also fosters innovation. Private companies and non-profits often have access to cutting-edge technologies, research, and best practices that can help governments address inefficiencies. For example, public-private partnerships (PPPs) have been used to deliver large-scale infrastructure projects more efficiently than traditional government-led initiatives.

Public-Private Partnerships (PPPs)

PPPs are agreements in which private companies and governments work together to finance, build, and operate public projects. These partnerships allow governments to leverage private sector expertise and funding while retaining oversight and accountability.

One successful example is the Indiana Toll Road project. Faced with financial difficulties, the state of Indiana leased the toll road to a private consortium, which agreed to operate and maintain it in exchange for toll revenues. The agreement provided the state with an upfront payment of $3.8 billion, which was reinvested in other infrastructure projects. While not without controversy, the PPP demonstrated how collaboration can address funding challenges and deliver public benefits.

To ensure that PPPs are successful, governments must establish clear contracts with measurable performance standards, transparent reporting requirements, and mechanisms for public oversight.

Nonprofit Partnerships for Public Services

Nonprofit organizations play a vital role in complementing government efforts, particularly in areas where resources are limited or specialized expertise is needed. Partnerships with nonprofits can enhance the delivery of public services, address social issues, and promote community engagement.

For example, the nonprofit organization Feeding America collaborates with federal programs like the Supplemental Nutrition Assistance Program (SNAP) to address food insecurity. By coordinating efforts and sharing resources, these partnerships expand access to food for vulnerable populations and reduce administrative costs.

Governments can strengthen these collaborations by providing funding, technical support, and platforms for information sharing. Clear communication and aligned goals are essential to ensuring that partnerships deliver meaningful results.

Citizen Advisory Councils

Citizen advisory councils provide a formal mechanism for public participation in government decision-making. These councils consist of community members who offer input on policies, programs, and budgets. Their insights help ensure that government actions reflect the needs and priorities of the people they serve.

For example, the city of Seattle established the Community Police Commission (CPC) to provide oversight and recommendations on police reform. The CPC works closely with city officials, law enforcement, and community organizations to address systemic issues and improve accountability. The commission's success has been attributed to its diverse membership, transparent processes, and commitment to collaboration.

Expanding the use of citizen advisory councils across sectors can enhance transparency and foster trust in government institutions.

Collaborative Budgeting Processes

Collaborative budgeting processes involve multiple stakeholders in the allocation of public funds. These processes ensure that budgets are aligned with community needs and reduce the risk of wasteful spending.

Participatory budgeting, discussed earlier, is one example of collaborative budgeting. Another approach is the use of stakeholder panels, which bring together representatives from government, business, and civil society to review and prioritize budget proposals.

For instance, the state of California convenes stakeholder panels to advise on the allocation of cap-and-trade revenues. These panels include representatives from environmental organizations, industry groups, and community advocates, ensuring that diverse perspectives are considered. The process has been credited with improving the effectiveness and equity of the state's climate investments.

The Role of Technology in Collaboration

Technology can facilitate collaboration by providing platforms for communication, data sharing, and decision-making. Online portals, virtual meetings, and collaborative software enable stakeholders to work together effectively, regardless of geographic location.

For example, the U.S. Department of Transportation's "Smart City Challenge" used an online platform to solicit ideas from cities across the country on how to improve transportation systems. The challenge encouraged collaboration between local governments, private companies, and academic institutions, resulting in innovative solutions that addressed congestion, safety, and sustainability.

Governments can further enhance collaboration by investing in digital infrastructure and providing training on the use of collaborative tools.

Challenges to Collaboration

While collaboration offers many benefits, it is not without challenges. Conflicting priorities, unequal power dynamics, and communication barriers can hinder the effectiveness of partnerships. To address these challenges, governments must:

Set Clear Expectations: Define roles, responsibilities, and goals for all participants to avoid misunderstandings.
Foster Mutual Respect: Acknowledge the expertise and contributions of all stakeholders and ensure that all voices are heard.
Build Trust: Establish transparent processes and accountability mechanisms to create confidence in the partnership.

Conclusion and Transition

Collaboration is essential for achieving fiscal responsibility and accountability in government spending. By working together, governments, private organizations, and citizens can address inefficiencies, reduce waste, and deliver better outcomes for communities.

In the next section, we will examine the role of education and public awareness in fostering a culture of accountability. By equipping citizens with the knowledge and tools they need to engage in governance, we can ensure that accountability becomes a shared responsibility.

Collaboration between governments, organizations, and citizens is only effective when paired with widespread public awareness and education. Informed citizens are better equipped to advocate for accountability, participate in decision-making, and hold officials responsible for wasteful spending. This page explores how education initiatives and public awareness campaigns can empower individuals and strengthen the culture of accountability.

The Importance of Public Awareness

Public awareness is a critical component of accountability. When citizens understand how government spending affects their daily lives, they are more likely to engage in advocacy efforts and demand responsible governance. Awareness campaigns also create a sense of shared responsibility, encouraging individuals to take an active role in monitoring and influencing public expenditures.

For example, campaigns highlighting the impact of wasteful spend-

ing on schools, healthcare, and infrastructure have successfully
mobilized communities to advocate for change. These efforts
demonstrate that when people see the tangible effects of mismanagement, they are more motivated to take action.

Educational Programs for Civic Engagement
Education is the foundation of an engaged and informed citizenry.
Governments, schools, and nonprofit organizations can collaborate
to provide educational programs that teach citizens about budgeting processes, fiscal policies, and advocacy strategies.

Workshops and Seminars: Hosting workshops on topics like government transparency, budget analysis, and advocacy techniques
can equip citizens with the skills they need to participate effectively
in governance.
School Curricula: Introducing civics education in schools can inspire
younger generations to take an interest in public affairs. Lessons on
topics such as taxes, government spending, and civic responsibility
prepare students to be active, informed citizens.
Community Forums: Public forums offer opportunities for citizens to
learn from experts, ask questions, and engage in discussions about
local and national issues.
For example, the state of Arizona's "Project Citizen" program involves middle and high school students in identifying and addressing community problems through research and policy proposals.
This hands-on approach fosters critical thinking and civic engagement from an early age.

Leveraging Media for Awareness Campaigns
Media outlets play a pivotal role in raising public awareness about
government spending. Investigative journalism, opinion pieces, and
televised debates can expose wasteful practices, educate the public, and influence policy discussions.

Investigative Reporting: Stories that uncover specific instances of
wasteful spending often spark public outrage and pressure policymakers to act. For instance, news coverage of the $43 million gas
station in Afghanistan brought the issue to national attention and
prompted investigations.
Public Service Announcements (PSAs): PSAs on television, radio,

and social media can highlight the importance of accountability and encourage citizens to get involved.

Documentaries and Films: Longer-form content, such as documentaries, can delve deeper into systemic issues and inspire viewers to advocate for change.

Collaborations between advocacy organizations and media outlets can amplify these efforts, ensuring that important stories reach broad audiences.

Harnessing Digital Platforms for Education

Digital platforms offer new opportunities for educating the public about accountability and government spending. Online resources, webinars, and interactive tools make it easier for individuals to access information and engage with complex topics.

Interactive Dashboards: Platforms like USAspending.gov allow citizens to explore government spending data in an accessible format. These tools empower users to investigate expenditures, identify inefficiencies, and share their findings.

Webinars and Online Courses: Organizations can host virtual events to educate participants about specific issues, such as budget oversight or advocacy strategies.

Gamification: Educational games and simulations, such as budget simulators, can make learning about fiscal responsibility engaging and interactive.

Community Outreach and Grassroots Engagement

While digital tools are valuable, face-to-face engagement remains essential for reaching underserved and disconnected communities. Grassroots outreach efforts, such as town hall meetings, canvassing, and door-to-door campaigns, help ensure that all citizens have the opportunity to participate in governance.

For example, a nonprofit organization might organize a series of community events to discuss local government spending and gather input on budget priorities. These events not only raise awareness but also build trust and foster a sense of ownership among participants.

The Role of Advocacy Organizations in Education

Advocacy organizations play a key role in educating the public about accountability. Many groups offer resources, training programs, and mentorship opportunities to help citizens become more effective advocates.

Toolkits and Guides: Organizations like the National Council of Nonprofits provide free resources that explain how to analyze budgets, track spending, and engage with policymakers.
Advocacy Training: Workshops and mentorship programs teach participants how to organize campaigns, communicate effectively, and influence policy decisions.
Public Awareness Campaigns: Advocacy groups often lead campaigns that combine education with calls to action, ensuring that citizens understand the issues and know how to get involved.
Measuring the Impact of Education Initiatives
To ensure the effectiveness of public awareness and education programs, it is important to measure their impact. Metrics such as participation rates, knowledge retention, and changes in civic engagement can provide valuable insights into what works and what doesn't.

For example, a city government might evaluate the success of its participatory budgeting program by tracking the number of residents who attend workshops, submit proposals, and vote on projects. Regular assessments help refine initiatives and ensure they continue to meet the needs of the community.

Conclusion and Transition
Education and public awareness are powerful tools for fostering a culture of accountability. By equipping citizens with the knowledge and skills they need to engage in governance, governments and organizations can build a more informed, active, and responsible public.

In the next section, we will examine how these efforts can be integrated into a broader strategy for systemic reform. By combining education, advocacy, and collaboration, we can create a government that prioritizes efficiency, transparency, and fiscal responsibility.

Creating a culture of accountability in government spending requires integrating education, advocacy, and collaboration into a unified strategy for systemic reform. This approach not only addresses immediate inefficiencies but also builds the foundation for long-term fiscal responsibility. In this section, we explore how these elements come together to form a comprehensive framework for improving governance.

Integrating Advocacy and Education

Advocacy and education are most effective when they are aligned and mutually reinforcing. While advocacy efforts mobilize citizens to demand change, education ensures that they are informed and equipped to participate meaningfully in governance. Integrating these elements creates a cycle of engagement that drives continuous improvement.

Advocacy Campaigns as Educational Tools: Advocacy campaigns can double as opportunities to educate the public. For instance, a campaign to eliminate wasteful spending in a specific program might include workshops or webinars that teach participants how to analyze budgets and track expenditures.

Educational Institutions as Advocates: Schools and universities can play a role in advocacy by promoting civic engagement and encouraging students to participate in campaigns. For example, a university might partner with a local government to develop a student-led initiative focused on improving transparency in public spending.

Community Partnerships: Collaborations between advocacy organizations and community groups can help ensure that educational programs reach diverse audiences. These partnerships provide opportunities to engage underrepresented populations and address their specific concerns.

Institutionalizing Accountability Mechanisms

Sustained accountability requires embedding mechanisms for oversight and transparency into the structure of government. These mechanisms ensure that reforms are not dependent on individual leaders or short-term initiatives but are maintained over time.

Independent Oversight Bodies: Establishing independent entities, such as auditors general or ethics commissions, provides an impartial check on government operations. These bodies can investigate waste, fraud, and abuse and recommend corrective actions.

Transparency Portals: Online platforms that publish real-time information about government spending empower citizens to monitor expenditures and hold officials accountable. By making this data accessible and user-friendly, governments can foster trust and encourage public participation.

Performance Metrics: Governments can adopt performance-based budgeting systems that tie funding to measurable outcomes. This approach incentivizes efficiency and ensures that taxpayer dollars are directed toward programs that deliver results.

Encouraging Innovation Through Collaboration

Collaboration between governments, private organizations, and citizens fosters innovation and enables stakeholders to tackle complex challenges more effectively. By sharing resources, expertise, and ideas, these partnerships can drive creative solutions to inefficiencies in public spending.

Innovation Labs: Government-sponsored innovation labs provide a space for testing new approaches to service delivery and budget management. These labs often involve collaboration with private companies, nonprofits, and academic institutions.

Crowdsourced Solutions: Platforms that solicit ideas from citizens can generate innovative solutions to public challenges. For example, a city government might launch a challenge to identify cost-saving measures in its transportation system, offering prizes for the best ideas.

Public-Private Partnerships: Partnering with private companies to deliver public projects, such as infrastructure improvements or technological upgrades, can reduce costs and improve efficiency.

Scaling Successful Models

Successful accountability initiatives often begin as pilot projects or localized efforts. Scaling these models to broader contexts requires careful planning and adaptation to different environments.

Evaluate and Adapt: Before scaling an initiative, it is important to assess its impact and identify lessons learned. Adjusting the model to address challenges and capitalize on strengths ensures that it is effective in new contexts.

Secure Buy-In: Scaling efforts often require support from multiple stakeholders, including policymakers, community leaders, and the public. Building consensus and securing commitments from key players are essential for success.

Leverage Networks: National and regional networks of governments and organizations provide a platform for sharing best practices and scaling successful initiatives. These networks facilitate collaboration and help align efforts across jurisdictions.

The Role of Leadership in Driving Change

Leadership is critical to fostering a culture of accountability. Government officials, advocacy leaders, and community organizers all have a role to play in setting the tone, promoting transparency, and inspiring action.

Championing Reforms: Leaders who advocate for accountability and fiscal responsibility can set an example for others to follow. Their commitment to ethical governance builds trust and encourages broader participation.

Empowering Teams: Effective leaders empower their teams by providing resources, support, and opportunities for professional development. This approach fosters innovation and ensures that reforms are implemented effectively.

Engaging the Public: Leaders who communicate openly and regularly with citizens create a sense of shared responsibility and strengthen the relationship between governments and the people they serve.

Conclusion and Transition

Collaboration, education, and advocacy are the cornerstones of a comprehensive strategy for improving accountability in government spending. By integrating these elements and scaling successful models, governments can create systems that prioritize efficiency, transparency, and public trust.

In the next chapter, we will explore the role of technology and data in driving systemic reform. From artificial intelligence to blockchain, emerging tools offer new possibilities for enhancing accountability and ensuring that taxpayer dollars are used effectively.

As governments face increasing demands for transparency and efficiency, emerging technologies and data-driven solutions offer powerful tools for enhancing accountability. From artificial intelligence to blockchain, these innovations have the potential to transform how governments operate, enabling more effective oversight and smarter use of taxpayer dollars. In this section, we explore how technology and data can be integrated into collaborative efforts to improve governance.

Artificial Intelligence (AI) in Governance
Artificial intelligence is revolutionizing industries worldwide, and its potential applications in government accountability are vast. By automating processes, analyzing large datasets, and detecting patterns, AI can help identify inefficiencies and prevent waste.

Fraud Detection: AI algorithms can analyze financial transactions to detect irregularities and flag potential cases of fraud or abuse. For example, machine learning models can identify duplicate claims or unusual spending patterns in government programs like Medicaid or unemployment benefits.
Predictive Analytics: Governments can use AI to forecast future spending needs and optimize resource allocation. Predictive models can help identify programs at risk of overspending and recommend corrective actions before issues arise.
Streamlining Administrative Tasks: Automation tools powered by AI can handle routine tasks, such as processing applications or managing payroll, freeing up staff to focus on more complex issues.
Blockchain for Transparency
Blockchain technology, best known for its use in cryptocurrencies, offers unique advantages for promoting transparency and accountability in government spending. By creating immutable, decentralized records, blockchain ensures that financial transactions are secure, verifiable, and tamper-proof.

Transparent Contracting: Governments can use blockchain to manage procurement processes, ensuring that contracts are awarded fairly and transparently. All bids, agreements, and payments can be recorded on the blockchain, making them accessible for public review.

Grant Management: Blockchain can streamline the disbursement of grants and aid by providing a transparent trail of how funds are allocated and spent. This reduces the risk of mismanagement and ensures that resources reach their intended recipients.

Taxpayer Tracking: Citizens could use blockchain-based systems to track how their tax dollars are spent, fostering trust and engagement.

Open Data and Analytics

Open data initiatives provide citizens, journalists, and advocacy organizations with access to government datasets, enabling them to analyze spending patterns and identify inefficiencies. Coupled with advanced analytics tools, open data can drive meaningful insights and inform policy decisions.

Visualization Tools: Platforms like Tableau and Microsoft Power BI allow users to create interactive dashboards that visualize spending data in an accessible format. These tools help uncover trends, outliers, and opportunities for improvement.

Public Dashboards: Governments can develop public-facing dashboards that display key performance metrics and financial data. For example, a dashboard showing the progress of infrastructure projects, complete with budget updates and timelines, can increase transparency and accountability.

Crowdsourced Analysis: By making datasets publicly available, governments can invite citizens and organizations to conduct their own analyses and contribute to oversight efforts.

Digital Collaboration Platforms

Collaboration tools enable governments, citizens, and organizations to work together more effectively, even across geographic boundaries. These platforms facilitate communication, document sharing, and project management, streamlining efforts to improve accountability.

Virtual Town Halls: Governments can use video conferencing platforms to host town hall meetings, engaging citizens in discussions about budget priorities and spending decisions.

Project Management Software: Tools like Trello or Asana can help manage collaborative initiatives, ensuring that tasks are assigned, deadlines are met, and progress is tracked.

Online Voting Systems: Digital platforms that enable citizens to vote on budget proposals or policy changes increase participation and make the decision-making process more inclusive.

Challenges and Risks of Technology

While technology offers significant benefits, it also comes with challenges and risks that must be addressed to ensure its effective use in governance.

Data Privacy: Governments must safeguard sensitive information to protect citizens' privacy while maintaining transparency.

Digital Divide: Access to technology varies widely among populations, creating potential inequities in who can participate in digital initiatives. Efforts to bridge this gap, such as providing internet access in underserved areas, are essential.

Algorithmic Bias: AI systems are only as good as the data they are trained on. Governments must ensure that algorithms are free from bias and produce fair, accurate results.

The Future of Accountability

The integration of technology and data into governance is transforming how governments operate and how citizens interact with public institutions. By embracing these tools, governments can enhance transparency, improve efficiency, and foster trust.

However, the success of these efforts depends on collaboration. Governments must work with private companies, advocacy organizations, and citizens to develop and implement technological solutions that align with public needs and values. By leveraging technology as a tool for collaboration, we can build a future where accountability is not just an ideal but a reality.

Conclusion and Transition

Technology and data are powerful allies in the fight against wasteful spending. By integrating these tools into collaborative efforts, governments can create systems that prioritize efficiency, transparency, and public trust.

In the next chapter, we will explore how these principles can be applied globally, examining case studies from other countries and identifying best practices that can inform efforts to improve accountability in the United States.

While technological innovations and collaborative strategies are essential for improving accountability, their application must also draw on lessons from global best practices. Governments worldwide face similar challenges in managing public funds, and some have implemented highly effective measures to reduce waste and improve transparency. By examining these successes, the United States can adopt strategies that align with its unique political and cultural context.

Case Study: Estonia's Digital Government
Estonia is often cited as a global leader in digital governance. Through its e-Estonia initiative, the country has created a fully integrated digital ecosystem that enables citizens and businesses to interact seamlessly with government services.

Digital Transparency: Estonia's online platforms allow citizens to view their tax data, monitor government spending, and participate in decision-making processes. This level of transparency has built trust and reduced opportunities for corruption.
Blockchain for Security: The country uses blockchain technology to secure its digital records, ensuring that data is tamper-proof and verifiable. This approach has been instrumental in fostering confidence in government operations.
Efficiency Gains: By digitizing nearly all government services, Estonia has significantly reduced administrative costs and improved service delivery.
The success of e-Estonia demonstrates the transformative potential of integrating technology into governance. While scaling such a system in the United States would require substantial investment and planning, elements like blockchain-based transparency tools and streamlined digital services could be adopted incrementally.

Case Study: Participatory Budgeting in Brazil
Participatory budgeting originated in Porto Alegre, Brazil, in the late 1980s and has since been implemented in cities around the world. This process allows citizens to propose and vote on how public funds should be allocated, fostering direct engagement and accountability.

Community Involvement: In Porto Alegre, citizens participate in annual assemblies to discuss budget priorities, submit project proposals, and vote on funding allocations.
Tangible Outcomes: The program has led to improved public infrastructure, such as paved roads and expanded sewer systems, while also increasing trust in local government.
Scalability: Participatory budgeting has been successfully replicated in cities of varying sizes and contexts, demonstrating its adaptability as a governance tool.
Incorporating participatory budgeting at the local level in the United States could empower communities, reduce waste, and ensure that public funds align with citizens' needs.

Case Study: South Korea's Open Data Initiatives
South Korea has made significant strides in improving government accountability through its commitment to open data. The government's Open Data Portal provides comprehensive access to datasets across sectors, enabling citizens and organizations to analyze and monitor public spending.

Citizen Empowerment: South Korea's open data initiatives allow citizens to track government expenditures, identify inefficiencies, and advocate for reforms.
Innovative Applications: Private companies and nonprofits have used open data to develop apps and tools that improve public services, such as traffic management systems and disaster response platforms.
Economic Benefits: The availability of open data has also spurred innovation and economic growth, creating new opportunities for businesses and entrepreneurs.
Expanding open data initiatives in the United States could similarly drive transparency, innovation, and public trust.

Learning from Global Challenges
While these examples highlight successes, they also offer lessons on the challenges of implementing accountability measures.

Cultural Resistance: In many countries, including the United States, resistance to change can hinder the adoption of new systems. Engaging stakeholders early and demonstrating the benefits of reforms can help overcome this barrier.

Equity Concerns: Digital initiatives must address disparities in access to technology and ensure that all citizens can participate. Tailored outreach efforts and investments in digital infrastructure are critical for inclusivity.

Balancing Transparency and Privacy: Governments must strike a balance between making data accessible and protecting sensitive information. Clear policies and robust security measures are essential to maintaining public trust.

Adapting Global Lessons to U.S. Context

The diverse political, economic, and cultural landscape of the United States requires tailored approaches to implementing global best practices. Strategies should focus on scalable, flexible solutions that can be adapted to local and national contexts.

Pilot Programs: Testing new initiatives on a small scale allows governments to refine strategies and address challenges before full implementation.

Public-Private Collaboration: Leveraging the expertise of private companies and nonprofits can accelerate the adoption of innovative solutions while ensuring alignment with public goals.

Federal-Local Partnerships: Collaborative efforts between federal and local governments can ensure that reforms address the unique needs of different communities.

Conclusion of Chapter 6

Collaboration, both within the United States and with international partners, is essential for fostering accountability and reducing wasteful spending. By learning from global best practices and adapting them to local contexts, the United States can build a governance system that prioritizes efficiency, transparency, and public trust.

In the next chapter, we will explore the future of fiscal responsibility, focusing on the policies, technologies, and cultural shifts needed to ensure that government spending serves the public good.

Chapter 7: The Future of Fiscal Responsibility

The future of fiscal responsibility in government spending hinges on a combination of policies, technologies, and cultural shifts that prioritize accountability, efficiency, and the public good. As governments face evolving challenges such as economic pressures, technological advancements, and changing societal expectations, they must adopt proactive strategies to ensure that public funds are managed wisely. This chapter explores the key elements that will define the path forward for fiscal responsibility.

Adopting Proactive Policies

The foundation of fiscal responsibility lies in adopting policies that prevent waste and ensure accountability. These policies must be forward-thinking, adaptable, and grounded in transparency.

Zero-Based Budgeting (ZBB): Unlike traditional budgeting, which builds on previous years' allocations, ZBB requires agencies to justify every expenditure from scratch. This approach encourages efficiency and eliminates automatic funding for outdated or redundant programs.

Spending Caps: Implementing caps on discretionary spending can help governments control costs and prioritize essential services. These caps should be accompanied by mechanisms to review and adjust limits based on economic conditions and public needs.

Regular Audits: Institutionalizing regular audits of government programs and agencies ensures ongoing accountability. Independent oversight bodies can identify inefficiencies and recommend improvements.

Leveraging Emerging Technologies

Technological advancements will play a critical role in shaping the future of fiscal responsibility. By embracing tools such as artificial intelligence, blockchain, and data analytics, governments can improve efficiency, reduce waste, and enhance transparency.

AI-Driven Decision Support: Artificial intelligence can analyze large datasets to provide insights into spending patterns, predict future needs, and identify opportunities for cost savings.

Blockchain for Accountability: Blockchain technology can create secure, transparent records of government transactions, reducing the risk of fraud and enabling citizens to track spending in real time.

Integrated Data Platforms: Centralized data platforms that consolidate information from multiple agencies can streamline operations, improve coordination, and enhance oversight.

Fostering a Culture of Accountability

Achieving fiscal responsibility requires a cultural shift within government institutions. Leaders and employees must embrace accountability as a core value and prioritize the efficient use of public funds.

Training and Development: Providing government employees with training on budgeting, ethics, and efficiency fosters a culture of responsibility. Workshops, seminars, and certification programs can enhance their skills and commitment.

Performance Incentives: Rewarding agencies and individuals for meeting efficiency goals or achieving measurable outcomes encourages responsible behavior and innovation.

Public Accountability Mechanisms: Creating opportunities for citizens to provide feedback on government spending reinforces the importance of transparency and responsiveness.

Engaging Citizens in Governance

The involvement of citizens is critical to sustaining fiscal responsibility. Engaged citizens hold governments accountable, advocate for reforms, and contribute to decision-making processes.

Participatory Budgeting: Expanding participatory budgeting programs at the local and national levels empowers citizens to have a direct say in how public funds are allocated.

Public Education Campaigns: Raising awareness about fiscal policies and government spending through educational campaigns ensures that citizens are informed and equipped to engage.

Feedback Loops: Establishing mechanisms for citizens to report inefficiencies or suggest improvements, such as online portals or community forums, fosters collaboration and trust.

Anticipating Future Challenges

As governments navigate the complexities of a rapidly changing world, they must anticipate and address emerging challenges that could impact fiscal responsibility.

Economic Uncertainty: Fluctuations in the global economy, such as recessions or inflation, require adaptive fiscal policies and contingency planning.

Technological Disruption: Advances in technology can create both opportunities and risks, necessitating a careful balance between innovation and regulation.

Demographic Shifts: Aging populations, urbanization, and migration trends will shape public spending priorities, requiring governments to adapt their strategies.

Conclusion and Transition

The future of fiscal responsibility depends on the collective efforts of governments, citizens, and organizations to embrace innovation, transparency, and collaboration. By adopting proactive policies, leveraging technology, fostering accountability, and engaging the public, governments can ensure that taxpayer dollars are used to serve the greater good.

In the next section, we will explore case studies of governments and organizations that are leading the way in fiscal responsibility. These examples provide inspiration and practical insights for building a more accountable and efficient system of governance.

As governments strive to build systems that prioritize fiscal responsibility, they can look to examples of success at various levels. Case studies from around the world illustrate how innovative approaches to governance, technology, and citizen engagement have led to significant improvements in accountability and efficiency. These examples provide a roadmap for how other governments can adopt and adapt similar strategies.

Case Study: New Zealand's Well-Being Budget

In 2019, New Zealand adopted a revolutionary approach to budgeting known as the Well-Being Budget. Unlike traditional budgets that focus solely on economic metrics like GDP, this framework prioritizes social, environmental, and cultural outcomes alongside fiscal performance.

Integrated Goals: The Well-Being Budget aligns spending with key priorities such as mental health, child poverty reduction, and climate change. Each allocation is evaluated based on its contribution to these outcomes.

Data-Driven Decision-Making: The budget process incorporates data and evidence to identify areas where investments will have the greatest impact on well-being.

Transparency and Accountability: By linking spending to specific outcomes, the Well-Being Budget provides clear benchmarks for success, enabling citizens to hold the government accountable.

This approach demonstrates how governments can redefine fiscal responsibility to encompass broader measures of public value. Adopting similar principles in the United States could help align federal, state, and local budgets with long-term societal goals.

Case Study: Denmark's Efficient Public Sector
Denmark consistently ranks as one of the most efficient public sectors in the world, thanks to its commitment to innovation, decentralization, and public engagement.

Innovation Labs: Denmark's public sector innovation labs test new approaches to service delivery, such as using artificial intelligence to streamline healthcare administration.

Decentralized Decision-Making: Local governments have significant autonomy in managing public services, which allows them to tailor solutions to community needs and operate more efficiently.

Citizen Involvement: The Danish government actively involves citizens in policy development, fostering trust and ensuring that services align with public priorities.

The Danish model highlights the importance of decentralization and collaboration in achieving fiscal responsibility. U.S. states and municipalities could benefit from adopting similar practices to empower local governments and improve service delivery.

Case Study: Canada's Open Government Initiative
Canada's Open Government Initiative aims to make government more transparent, accountable, and collaborative through open data and public engagement.

Comprehensive Open Data Portal: Canada's open data platform provides access to thousands of datasets, enabling citizens to explore government spending, policy outcomes, and more.

Public Consultations: The government regularly seeks input from citizens on major initiatives, such as climate policies and budget priorities.
Performance Reporting: Canada publishes detailed reports on the progress of its commitments, ensuring accountability and enabling continuous improvement.
This initiative underscores the potential of transparency to drive accountability and foster trust. Expanding open government practices in the United States could enhance citizen engagement and improve oversight of public spending.

Case Study: Local Success in the U.S. - Austin, Texas
Austin, Texas, has emerged as a leader in participatory governance, using innovative approaches to engage citizens and improve fiscal responsibility.

Participatory Budgeting: The city's participatory budgeting program allows residents to propose and vote on projects funded by a portion of the city's budget. This initiative has funded improvements such as park upgrades and public art installations.
Data-Driven Policies: Austin uses data analytics to optimize public services, such as reducing traffic congestion and improving waste management.
Transparency Tools: The city's online budget portal provides residents with detailed information about expenditures and project outcomes.
Austin's success demonstrates the value of combining citizen engagement, data-driven decision-making, and transparency to achieve better governance at the local level.

Scaling and Adapting Success Stories
While these case studies highlight diverse approaches to fiscal responsibility, their common themes include innovation, transparency, and citizen engagement. To scale these successes, governments must:

Encourage Experimentation: Pilot programs allow governments to test new ideas and refine them before full implementation.
Invest in Training: Providing officials with the skills and knowledge needed to adopt innovative practices ensures the sustainability of

reforms.
Foster Collaboration: Partnerships between governments, nonprofits, and the private sector can accelerate the adoption of successful models.
Conclusion and Transition
These examples illustrate that fiscal responsibility is not just about cutting costs—it's about delivering value to citizens through efficient, transparent, and responsive governance. By learning from global and local successes, governments can build systems that meet the challenges of the future while earning the trust of the people they serve.

In the next section, we will examine potential roadblocks to achieving fiscal responsibility and strategies for overcoming them. From political resistance to systemic inertia, understanding these challenges is essential for driving lasting change.

While examples of success provide a roadmap for improving fiscal responsibility, the path forward is not without obstacles. Achieving meaningful and lasting change requires overcoming a range of challenges, from political resistance and systemic inertia to public skepticism and resource limitations. This section explores these barriers and outlines strategies for addressing them effectively.

Challenge 1: Political Resistance
Political resistance often stems from competing priorities, entrenched interests, or a reluctance to disrupt established systems. Elected officials may hesitate to support reforms that could be perceived as unpopular, particularly if they involve reallocating funds from well-established programs.

Strategies for Addressing Political Resistance:

Build Coalitions: Advocacy groups, community leaders, and private sector allies can create unified pressure on policymakers to support fiscal reforms.
Highlight Public Demand: Demonstrating widespread public support through petitions, polls, or town hall meetings can encourage politicians to take action.
Frame Reforms Positively: Emphasizing the benefits of fiscal re-

sponsibility, such as improved services or reduced waste, can help garner political backing.

Challenge 2: Systemic Inertia

Bureaucratic systems are often resistant to change, even when inefficiencies are widely acknowledged. Processes that have been in place for decades can be difficult to overhaul, particularly in large, complex organizations.

Strategies for Combating Systemic Inertia:

Start Small: Pilot programs can demonstrate the feasibility and benefits of new approaches, building momentum for broader reforms.

Invest in Change Management: Training programs and clear communication can help employees adapt to new systems and processes.

Leverage Leadership: Reform-minded leaders can set the tone and drive initiatives forward, inspiring others to follow suit.

Challenge 3: Public Skepticism

Public trust in government is often low, particularly when wasteful spending or corruption has been widely reported. This skepticism can hinder efforts to engage citizens in reform initiatives.

Strategies for Building Public Trust:

Transparency: Providing clear, accessible information about government spending and reform efforts can rebuild trust.

Engagement: Involving citizens in decision-making processes, such as participatory budgeting or public consultations, demonstrates a commitment to accountability.

Celebrating Success: Highlighting examples of successful reforms and their tangible benefits can inspire confidence in future initiatives.

Challenge 4: Resource Limitations

Implementing reforms often requires upfront investments in technology, training, or personnel. Limited budgets can make it challenging to allocate resources for these initiatives, particularly during economic downturns.

Strategies for Overcoming Resource Constraints:

Prioritize High-Impact Reforms: Focus on initiatives that offer the greatest return on investment, such as reducing fraud or streamlining procurement.

Leverage Partnerships: Collaborations with private companies or nonprofits can provide additional resources and expertise.

Seek Grants or Loans: Funding from international organizations or philanthropic foundations can support reform efforts, particularly in resource-limited contexts.

Challenge 5: Balancing Competing Priorities

Governments must balance fiscal responsibility with the need to address pressing social, economic, and environmental challenges. Focusing too narrowly on cost-cutting can undermine investments in critical areas, such as education or healthcare.

Strategies for Achieving Balance:

Adopt Holistic Metrics: Using frameworks like New Zealand's Well-Being Budget ensures that spending decisions consider social and environmental outcomes alongside economic factors.

Engage Stakeholders: Collaborating with community organizations, advocacy groups, and industry leaders can help identify priorities and allocate resources effectively.

Plan for the Long Term: Developing multi-year budgets and strategic plans ensures that short-term savings do not come at the expense of long-term goals.

Opportunities in Overcoming Challenges

While these challenges are significant, they also present opportunities for innovation and collaboration. By addressing resistance, inertia, skepticism, resource constraints, and competing priorities head-on, governments can create systems that are not only fiscally responsible but also more equitable and responsive to public needs.

Conclusion and Transition

Overcoming the barriers to fiscal responsibility requires persistence, collaboration, and a willingness to embrace change. In the next section, we will summarize the key principles of effective governance explored throughout this book and provide actionable recommendations for policymakers, advocacy organizations, and citizens.

As we approach the conclusion of this chapter, it is important to consolidate the lessons learned and outline actionable steps for achieving fiscal responsibility. Governments, advocacy organizations, and citizens all play critical roles in this process, and their collaboration can create a system that prioritizes efficiency, transparency, and public trust. This section synthesizes the key principles discussed throughout the book and provides a roadmap for moving forward.

Key Principles for Fiscal Responsibility
Transparency as a Foundation
Transparency is the cornerstone of accountability. Governments must provide clear, accessible, and comprehensive information about spending decisions, outcomes, and challenges.

Expand open data initiatives to ensure that spending information is available in real time.
Develop interactive dashboards and platforms to make data accessible to all citizens.
Encourage media and advocacy groups to analyze and disseminate spending information.
Citizen Engagement and Participation
Engaging citizens in governance ensures that spending decisions align with public needs and priorities.

Implement participatory budgeting programs at local, state, and national levels.
Host public consultations and forums to gather input on budget priorities.
Create mechanisms for citizens to report inefficiencies and suggest improvements.
Innovation and Technology
Leveraging technology can enhance efficiency, reduce waste, and improve accountability.

Use artificial intelligence and data analytics to identify inefficiencies and forecast spending needs.
Adopt blockchain for secure and transparent financial transactions.
Invest in digital tools and platforms that streamline government

operations.

Collaboration Across Sectors

Partnerships between governments, private organizations, and non-profits can provide additional resources, expertise, and innovative solutions.

Foster public-private partnerships to deliver infrastructure projects and technological upgrades.

Collaborate with advocacy groups and community organizations to promote accountability and citizen engagement.

Encourage academic institutions to conduct research and provide insights into best practices.

Performance-Driven Policies

Policies should prioritize measurable outcomes and align spending with long-term goals.

Implement performance-based budgeting to tie funding to results.

Conduct regular audits and evaluations to identify areas for improvement.

Use frameworks like New Zealand's Well-Being Budget to balance economic, social, and environmental objectives.

Recommendations for Policymakers

Policymakers have the power to drive systemic change by enacting reforms that promote accountability and fiscal responsibility. Key recommendations include:

Enacting legislation that mandates transparency in government spending.

Providing funding and support for innovation labs and pilot programs.

Establishing independent oversight bodies to monitor spending and investigate inefficiencies.

Recommendations for Advocacy Organizations

Advocacy groups play a vital role in holding governments accountable and educating the public. Recommendations include:

Launching campaigns that highlight instances of wasteful spending and advocate for reforms.

Building coalitions to amplify impact and align efforts across organizations.

Offering training programs and resources to empower citizens to engage in advocacy.
Recommendations for Citizens
Citizens are the backbone of accountability, and their involvement is essential for driving change. Recommendations include:

Staying informed about government spending through resources like open data portals and watchdog reports.
Participating in local governance initiatives, such as town halls and participatory budgeting programs.
Advocating for transparency and accountability by contacting elected officials and supporting reform efforts.
The Path Forward
Fiscal responsibility is not an endpoint but an ongoing process that requires vigilance, innovation, and collaboration. By embracing the principles and recommendations outlined in this book, governments and citizens can work together to create a system that serves the public good and earns public trust.

Conclusion and Transition
The final chapter will summarize the core themes of this book, reflecting on the transformative potential of fiscal responsibility and offering a call to action for all stakeholders to play their part in building a better future.

Chapter 8: A Call to Action

The journey toward fiscal responsibility is not merely a policy ambition—it is a moral imperative and a societal necessity. Wasteful spending erodes public trust, diverts resources from pressing needs, and perpetuates inefficiencies that stifle progress. Yet, the tools, strategies, and case studies presented throughout this book demonstrate that meaningful change is possible. As we conclude, this chapter consolidates the insights and principles discussed, providing a comprehensive call to action for all stakeholders—policymakers, advocacy organizations, and citizens alike.

The Critical Importance of Fiscal Responsibility
Fiscal responsibility is more than an abstract ideal; it is a tangible mechanism for societal improvement. Responsible management of taxpayer dollars allows governments to:

Address critical social needs, such as education, healthcare, and infrastructure.
Maintain public trust and demonstrate ethical stewardship.
Ensure economic sustainability and resilience against financial crises.
Neglecting fiscal responsibility not only squanders resources but also undermines democratic values, as citizens lose faith in institutions that fail to manage funds effectively.

The Core Pillars of Fiscal Responsibility
Throughout this book, several recurring themes have emerged as foundational to achieving accountability in government spending. These pillars serve as a roadmap for systemic reform:

Transparency:
Transparency is the bedrock of trust. Governments must adopt open data practices, providing citizens with real-time access to spending information. Transparency fosters accountability, enabling the public to monitor expenditures and identify inefficiencies.

Citizen Engagement:
Active participation by citizens ensures that spending aligns with

public priorities. Mechanisms such as participatory budgeting and public consultations empower individuals to influence decisions and hold officials accountable.

Innovation:
Leveraging technology, such as artificial intelligence, blockchain, and advanced data analytics, can revolutionize how governments manage resources. These tools enhance efficiency, reduce waste, and provide new avenues for oversight.

Collaboration:
Partnerships between governments, private entities, and nonprofit organizations amplify the impact of reform efforts. Collaborative approaches pool expertise and resources, driving creative solutions to systemic challenges.

Performance Metrics:
Governments must adopt performance-based budgeting systems, linking funding to measurable outcomes. This approach ensures that taxpayer dollars are used effectively and that programs deliver tangible benefits.

The Stakes for Policymakers, Advocates, and Citizens
Each stakeholder group has a unique role to play in advancing fiscal responsibility. Success requires coordinated efforts, a shared commitment to ethical governance, and a willingness to embrace change.

The Role of Policymakers in Driving Reform
Policymakers hold the greatest responsibility in shaping a culture of fiscal responsibility. Their decisions directly influence how public funds are allocated, managed, and accounted for. As stewards of taxpayer dollars, they must prioritize efficiency and transparency in every aspect of governance.

Key Actions for Policymakers:

Institutionalize Transparency Mechanisms:

Enact laws mandating open data platforms that provide real-time

insights into government spending.
Require detailed reporting on the outcomes of funded programs and initiatives.
Adopt Performance-Based Budgeting:

Transition from traditional incremental budgeting to systems that tie funding to measurable outcomes.
Ensure that programs demonstrate value and align with public priorities to justify continued support.
Champion Ethical Governance:

Commit to rejecting pork-barrel spending and earmarks that prioritize political interests over public benefit.
Foster a culture of integrity within government institutions by holding officials accountable for misuse of funds.
The Role of Advocacy Organizations in Building Momentum
Advocacy organizations play a crucial role in uncovering inefficiencies, raising awareness, and mobilizing public support for reforms. They act as watchdogs, educators, and catalysts for change, bridging the gap between citizens and government institutions.

Key Actions for Advocacy Organizations:

Expose Wasteful Spending:

Use investigative research to identify instances of waste, fraud, or mismanagement.
Publish accessible reports and visualizations that resonate with the public and policymakers alike.
Empower Citizens Through Education:

Develop toolkits, workshops, and online resources that teach citizens how to analyze budgets and engage in advocacy.
Partner with schools and universities to incorporate fiscal responsibility into civic education.
Collaborate for Greater Impact:

Build coalitions with other organizations to align messaging and amplify campaigns.
Partner with media outlets to reach broader audiences and maintain

public pressure on government institutions.
The Role of Citizens in Driving Accountability
Citizens are the foundation of democratic governance, and their engagement is essential for sustaining accountability. By staying informed and participating in governance, individuals can ensure that their voices shape how public funds are used.

Key Actions for Citizens:

Engage in Local Governance:

Attend town hall meetings, participate in public consultations, and advocate for participatory budgeting initiatives.
Contact elected officials to express concerns about wasteful spending or advocate for transparency reforms.
Leverage Technology for Oversight:

Use open data platforms and transparency tools to monitor government spending and report inefficiencies.
Share findings with community members and advocacy organizations to build collective action.
Support Accountability Movements:

Join or donate to organizations dedicated to fiscal responsibility.
Vote for candidates who prioritize transparency, accountability, and ethical governance.
The Interconnected Roles of Stakeholders
The efforts of policymakers, advocacy organizations, and citizens are interconnected, and their collaboration is critical for lasting change. Policymakers rely on public pressure to enact reforms, advocacy organizations depend on citizen engagement to amplify their campaigns, and citizens need access to transparent information and ethical leadership to participate meaningfully.

The Role of Technology in Advancing Fiscal Responsibility
Technology serves as both an enabler and a catalyst for improving fiscal accountability. When leveraged effectively, it can transform governance by making processes more efficient, accessible, and transparent.

Key Technological Innovations for Fiscal Responsibility:

Artificial Intelligence (AI) and Machine Learning:

Fraud Detection: AI can analyze spending patterns to identify anomalies, reducing fraud in programs such as Medicaid or unemployment insurance.
Predictive Analytics: Machine learning models can forecast budgetary needs, helping governments allocate resources more effectively.
Blockchain for Transparent Spending:

Immutable Records: Blockchain technology ensures that financial transactions are secure and verifiable, preventing tampering and corruption.
Real-Time Tracking: Governments can use blockchain to provide citizens with live updates on how public funds are spent.
Open Data Portals:

Platforms like USAspending.gov allow citizens to explore government expenditures in user-friendly formats, fostering transparency and public engagement.
Expanding these platforms to include detailed project timelines and performance metrics can further enhance their utility.
Crowdsourcing Platforms:

Citizens can use tools like SeeClickFix to report inefficiencies or suggest improvements in public services.
Governments can solicit ideas for cost-saving measures or innovative solutions through online challenges and hackathons.
Cultural Shifts Toward Accountability
Achieving fiscal responsibility requires not only structural reforms but also a cultural transformation within government institutions and society at large. This shift involves redefining success in governance to emphasize ethical stewardship, efficiency, and public trust.

Encouraging Cultural Change:

Within Government:

Promote a mindset of "results-driven governance," where funding decisions are based on measurable outcomes rather than political priorities.
Provide training programs that equip public officials with skills in budget management, data analysis, and ethical decision-making.
Among Citizens:

Foster a culture of civic engagement by emphasizing the importance of monitoring and participating in governance.
Recognize and celebrate individuals and communities that successfully advocate for transparency and accountability.
Through Leadership:

Leaders must exemplify fiscal responsibility in their actions and decisions, setting a standard for others to follow.
Publicly acknowledge and address inefficiencies, demonstrating a commitment to continuous improvement.
Overcoming Barriers to Reform
The journey toward fiscal responsibility is not without obstacles.
Political resistance, systemic inertia, and limited resources can hinder progress, but these challenges are surmountable with strategic planning and collective action.

Strategies for Overcoming Barriers:

Build Momentum Through Quick Wins:

Start with reforms that yield immediate, visible results, such as eliminating redundant programs or improving procurement processes.
Engage Stakeholders Early:

Involve citizens, advocacy groups, and private sector partners in the design and implementation of reforms to ensure buy-in and alignment.
Secure Long-Term Commitments:

Establish policies and practices that institutionalize accountability mechanisms, ensuring they persist beyond changes in leadership or political cycles.
The Ripple Effect of Fiscal Responsibility

When governments prioritize fiscal responsibility, the benefits extend far beyond immediate cost savings. Responsible spending fosters public trust, enhances the quality of public services, and strengthens democratic institutions. It also inspires other nations and organizations to adopt similar practices, creating a global movement toward accountability and transparency.

The Ripple Effects of Fiscal Responsibility

When governments commit to fiscal responsibility, the impact resonates far beyond immediate financial outcomes. Responsible spending can transform the relationship between citizens and their government, demonstrating that public institutions are ethical stewards of taxpayer dollars. This transformation leads to a cascade of positive effects:

Enhanced Public Trust:

Transparency and accountability rebuild confidence in government institutions. Citizens who see their taxes used effectively are more likely to engage in governance and support public initiatives.

Strengthened Democracy:

Fiscal responsibility ensures that resources are allocated equitably, addressing societal needs and promoting fairness. A government that prioritizes efficiency over waste reinforces democratic values and strengthens the social contract.

Global Leadership:

Nations that demonstrate fiscal accountability set a standard for others to follow. By sharing best practices and fostering international collaboration, governments can contribute to a global culture of responsible governance.

A Unified Strategy for All Stakeholders

Achieving fiscal responsibility requires a unified strategy that aligns the efforts of policymakers, advocacy organizations, and citizens. Each group brings unique strengths and perspectives to the table, and their collaboration is essential for sustainable reform.

Core Elements of a Unified Strategy:

Integrated Platforms for Collaboration:

Create digital hubs where policymakers, advocates, and citizens can share ideas, data, and progress updates.
Use these platforms to coordinate initiatives, streamline processes, and foster a sense of shared responsibility.
Cross-Sector Partnerships:

Encourage partnerships between governments, businesses, non-profits, and academic institutions to pool resources and expertise.
Focus on joint projects that address systemic inefficiencies and promote innovation.
Regular Monitoring and Evaluation:

Establish mechanisms to track the implementation and outcomes of reforms.
Use data-driven insights to refine strategies and ensure that goals are met.
Building Momentum for Change
Momentum is critical for sustaining reform efforts and overcoming resistance. By focusing on quick wins and visible successes, stakeholders can build confidence and generate public support for broader initiatives.

Strategies for Building Momentum:

Highlight Tangible Benefits:

Showcase examples of programs or initiatives that have saved money, improved services, or increased transparency.
Use storytelling and testimonials to demonstrate the real-world impact of fiscal responsibility.
Leverage Media and Social Platforms:

Use traditional and digital media to amplify the message of accountability and engage diverse audiences.
Encourage citizens to share their experiences and advocate for change through social networks.
Celebrate Successes:

Recognize individuals, organizations, and governments that exemplify fiscal responsibility.
Host events or awards ceremonies to celebrate milestones and inspire others to follow suit.
Sustaining Long-Term Reform
While initial successes are important, the ultimate goal is to create a culture of accountability that endures over time. This requires institutionalizing reforms and fostering a mindset of continuous improvement.

Key Actions for Sustaining Reform:

Codify Accountability Mechanisms:

Pass laws and regulations that embed transparency and performance metrics into government operations.
Promote Education and Training:

Invest in ongoing education programs for policymakers, public officials, and citizens to reinforce the principles of fiscal responsibility.
Adapt to Emerging Challenges:

Continuously evaluate the impact of reforms and adapt strategies to address new challenges, such as economic downturns or technological disruptions.
A Vision for the Future
The vision of a fiscally responsible government is one where every dollar spent contributes to the public good, every decision is grounded in data and ethics, and every citizen has a voice in governance. This vision is ambitious but attainable, and its realization depends on the collective efforts of all stakeholders.

A Blueprint for Moving Forward
As we close the discussion on fiscal responsibility, it is essential to provide a blueprint for turning principles into action. By focusing on concrete steps, all stakeholders can contribute to creating a governance system that prioritizes efficiency, transparency, and accountability.

For Policymakers:

Commit to enacting and enforcing laws that promote fiscal responsibility, such as transparency mandates and performance-based budgeting.
Foster a culture of innovation within government by supporting pilot programs and adopting successful practices from other nations and communities.
Collaborate across political lines to ensure that reforms are comprehensive and sustainable.
For Advocacy Organizations:

Focus campaigns on specific, actionable goals, such as increasing public access to budget data or eliminating redundant programs.
Use storytelling and data to connect with audiences and build widespread support for reforms.
Partner with civic organizations, media outlets, and academic institutions to amplify the impact of advocacy efforts.
For Citizens:

Educate yourself about government budgets, spending processes, and advocacy strategies. Knowledge is power in holding officials accountable.
Participate in local governance by attending meetings, engaging in public consultations, and supporting participatory budgeting programs.
Vote for leaders who prioritize transparency and ethical governance, and hold them accountable throughout their terms.
The Transformative Potential of Accountability
Fiscal responsibility is not an isolated goal—it is a transformative force that can reshape governance and society as a whole. By managing public funds wisely, governments can:

Deliver high-quality services that meet the needs of all citizens.
Reduce inequality by prioritizing investments in underserved communities.
Strengthen democratic institutions by fostering trust and engagement.
A Shared Responsibility
The success of fiscal reforms depends on the shared responsibility of all stakeholders. Governments must lead with integrity and

innovation, advocacy organizations must act as watchdogs and educators, and citizens must remain vigilant and engaged. Together, these efforts can create a governance system that reflects the highest ideals of democracy.

A Call to Action
This is not just a moment for reflection but a call to action. Whether you are a policymaker, advocate, or citizen, your role in promoting fiscal responsibility matters. The tools and strategies outlined in this book provide a foundation for action, but it is up to each of us to ensure they are implemented and sustained.

To Policymakers:
Lead with courage and conviction. Recognize that fiscal responsibility is not just about numbers—it is about serving the public good and earning the trust of those you represent.

To Advocacy Organizations:
Continue to shine a light on inefficiencies and wasteful spending. Use your platforms to educate, mobilize, and inspire citizens to demand better governance.

To Citizens:
Your voice is your power. Engage in the democratic process, hold officials accountable, and advocate for reforms that reflect your values and priorities.

Looking to the Future
The journey toward fiscal responsibility is challenging, but the rewards are profound. A government that manages its resources responsibly not only strengthens its democracy but also creates a better future for its citizens.

Let this be a starting point for action. Together, we can build a system of governance that embodies efficiency, accountability, and transparency—a system that works for everyone.

References:

The following references were used in the creation of Government Wasteful Spending: A Taxpayer's Nightmare by Samuel Carter. These sources provide detailed evidence, case studies, and expert analysis on the topic of wasteful government spending and reforms for accountability. Readers are encouraged to explore these materials for further study.

Government Reports and Watchdog Analyses
Government Accountability Office (GAO):

Annual performance and accountability reports.
Specific audits on federal agency inefficiencies and waste.
Available at gao.gov.
Senator Rand Paul's "Festivus Report":

Annual report highlighting wasteful federal spending across various agencies.
Comprehensive breakdown of specific projects and their costs.
Citizens Against Government Waste (CAGW):

"The Pig Book": A detailed account of pork-barrel spending in federal budgets.
Available at cagw.org.
Office of Inspector General Reports:

Various reports on fraud and abuse in Medicare, Medicaid, and other federal programs.
Available at oig.hhs.gov.
Case Studies and News Articles
The Shrimp on a Treadmill Research:

Coverage from The Washington Post, detailing the controversy around NSF-funded research projects.
Article title: "The Real Story Behind Shrimp on a Treadmill."
The $43 Million Gas Station in Afghanistan:

Investigation by the Special Inspector General for Afghanistan Reconstruction (SIGAR).

Detailed in SIGAR Quarterly Report to Congress, 2015.
Fraud in Pandemic Relief Programs:

Reporting by ProPublica on widespread abuse of Paycheck Protection Program (PPP) loans.
Available at propublica.org.
Academic Research and Publications
Performance-Based Budgeting in Public Administration:

Author: Robert D. Behn
Title: Rethinking Democratic Accountability.
Publisher: Brookings Institution Press.
Transparency and Open Government:

Author: Beth Simone Noveck
Title: Wiki Government: How Technology Can Make Government Better, Democracy Stronger, and Citizens More Powerful.
Publisher: Brookings Institution Press.
Public Budgeting and Financial Management:

Author: Irene S. Rubin
Title: The Politics of Public Budgeting: Getting and Spending, Borrowing and Balancing.
Publisher: CQ Press.
Global Examples and Best Practices
Participatory Budgeting in Porto Alegre, Brazil:
Source: World Bank case study on participatory governance.
Title: "Porto Alegre's Participatory Budget: A Model for Urban Management."
Digital Governance in Estonia:
Source: e-Estonia Briefing Centre publications.
Available at e-estonia.com.
Canada's Open Government Initiative:
Source: Canadian Open Data Portal.
Available at open.canada.ca.
Additional Suggested Reading
Economic Consequences of Government Waste:
Author: David A. Stockman
Title: The Triumph of Politics: Why the Reagan Revolution Failed.
The Role of Watchdogs in Governance:

Author: Paul Light
Title: Monitoring Government: Inspectors General and the Search
for Accountability.
Publisher: Brookings Institution Press.
The Ethics of Public Spending:
Author: Michael Walzer
Title: Spheres of Justice: A Defense of Pluralism and Equality.
Publisher: Basic Books.